HOTFOOT TO ZABRISKIE POINT

A UNIPART CALENDAR BOOK

· HOTFOOT TO · ZABRISKIE POINT

JILLY COOPER AND PATRICK LICHFIELD

CONSTABLE · LONDON

First published in Great Britain 1985
by Constable and Company Limited
10 Orange Street, London WC2H 7EG
Copyright photographs © by Unipart Ltd 1985
text © by Jilly Cooper 1985

ISBN 0 09 466760 8

Designed by Ashted Dastor
The black and white photographs in
this book were taken by Chalky Whyte
Set in Bodoni by
Servis Filmsetting Ltd, Manchester
Printed and bound in Great Britain
by W.S. Cowell Ltd, Ipswich

THE FILM CREW.

CLIVE   KEITH

DIR/PROD.   CAMERA.

PETER.   PAUL
GRIP.   SOUND.

AISHA.

Mysterious Beauty from the EAST

Paula

Mysterious Beauty. Known to treat.

PAULA

Mysterious beauty from Bonn really rich

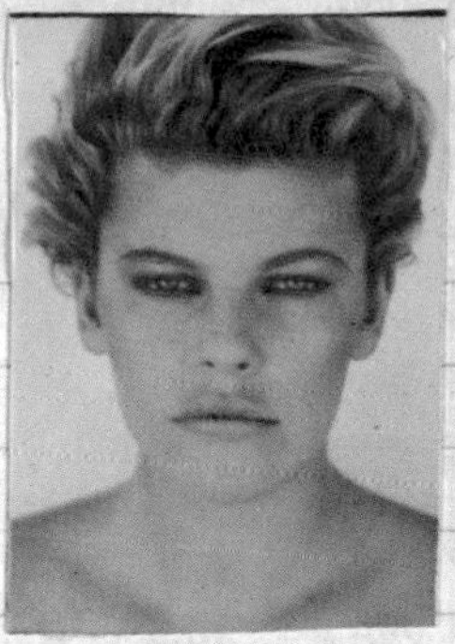

"Excellent"

LOOPER TROOPER

Lewis in Disguise

"Comic"

Tilly COOPER.

Dr Jamie Bellamy is disguise

Rom Anti-car

A.K.A CHETRE Ancien.

Knows about Bull Rays

CHALKS (Rif:) Whyte
(mostly undercovers)

(Second hand shaggy legs)

"Guvnor"
(Grumpy)

"Grumpy over eazey"
(J.C.)

(Considering an overtime job)

Pedro ("Rae") Kaine (Prob. C.I.A)

Only 1/3 strapping

Fix the Marshall Jr bastion — Lady Keep

Scissors — Jackie.

DRAMATICALLY

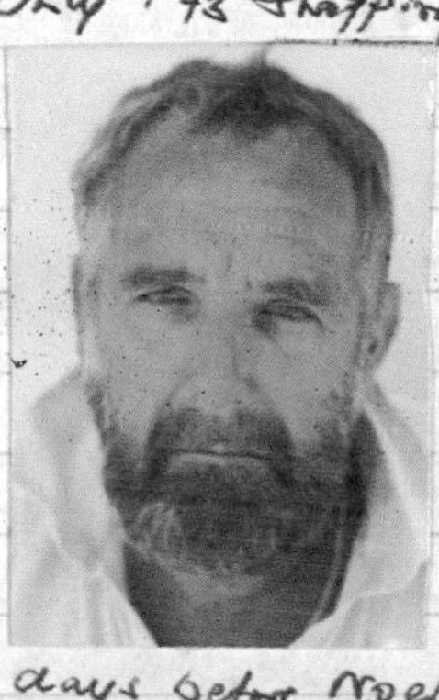

days before noel.

Best at JHABA.

Dramatically scorches

Clayton Pl.

CLAYTON HOWARD.
(specially warpaint)

Saturday 18 May, Gloucestershire

Return drenched and frozen from walking the dogs through the fields before breakfast. Find letter from Constable, the publishers, asking whether I would like to go to Mexico for a fortnight and write a book about Lord Lichfield photographing three models for the 1986 Unipart Calendar? Am fed up with lousy English summer, and was captivated by Patrick Lichfield when he joined the panel of 'What's My Line?' recently, so I accept with alacrity.

Spend afternoon getting four large books on Mexico out of library and pinning thirty-one-day pre-Unipart-Calendar-trip crash diet on the fridge door so I won't look too gross by comparison with the models.

Friday 9 June

So far failed to stick to diet, but at least dazzlingly briefed on Mexico. Join everyone who's going on the trip for a briefing breakfast at the Carlton Towers. All of them, except the models, have worked on the Calendar before. Gossip whizzes back and forth like a Wimbledon final. Everyone is very bullish because last year's Unipart Calendar, shot in Bali, has just won the Kodak Award for Calendar Photography.

The models, all ravishing, a blonde and two brunettes, sit up the other end of the table, holding their knives like pencils and tucking into shiny black mushrooms, bacon and eggs, and waffles and maple syrup.

The blonde, Paula, aged nineteen, has turquoise eyes, blonde hair slicked back like Rudolph Valentino, the disturbingly androgynous looks of a Greek youth, and a Black Country accent.

One of the brunettes, Gloria, is twenty-four and one of the most beautiful girls I have ever seen, with black curls, huge brown eyes and pink lips like a plunger. Her mother is Welsh, she says, and her father is Jamaican and as black as the ace of spades. They met when they were both at Trinity, Dublin.

The other brunette, Aysha, who is twenty-three, has Charles II hair, as though she'd whisked it with an egg beater, and delicate parasol-protected looks. She says she is half Turkish, and her boyfriend took her somewhere warm earlier in the year but she can't remember where it was. They all have a curious passivity about them, like Renoir nudes being shipped abroad for an exhibition.

Patrick Lichfield arrives late, with bags under his eyes, saying he's got 'flu, and proceeds to eat a large breakfast. Realize all the other men in the party have beards, like disciples. How will I ever distinguish them?

Turn to the beard on my left, and start animatedly talking about Mexican myths, only to be told we are not going to Mexico after all. Two of the other beards evidently spent £7,000 on a recce there, only to find that it was not good-looking enough, and that they would run into insuperable problems trying to photograph nudes in a predominantly Catholic country, so they decided to change the location.

'Excuse me,' says Paula the Greek youth, in her Black Country accent, 'could you tell me where I'm actually going?'

A dramatic-looking woman, with jet-black hair and an aquiline nose, rises at the end of the table.

'Death Valley,' she says slowly.

There is a long pause.

The woman, who turns out to be Jackie Cryer, the stylist who provides the props and the models' clothes for the trip, proceeds to give us all, but mostly the models, a daunting pep talk.

'It's going to be incredibly hot in Death Valley. Temperatures go up to 135 in the shade, so we'll only be able to shoot early in the morning and at sunset. You're bound to get allergies, and you mustn't get too much sun or you'll look awful. Nor do we want you teetering over the rocks in high heels, so make sure you've got shoes with thick soles, or they'll melt. And you must be constantly on the look-out for scorpions, tarantulas and snakes.'

The models turn pale. Phobic about snakes, I rush shrieking to ring my agent, only to discover I have already signed the contract.

Monday 17 June

So worried about snakes, I've actually put on two pounds misery-eating on my crash diet. Am just packing thigh boots when my son, who is taking O-levels, rings up to say Death Valley is where the Americans explode all their nuclear bombs, and I'll probably die from fallout. Contemplate packing gas mask.

Paula
Gloria
Aysha

In the evening Leo, my husband, and I – miserable at the prospect of separation – have inevitable row, as he warns me of the culture shock, the punishing heat, and the cauldron of rows, feuds and jealousies into which I am about to be catapulted.

In the middle my mother rings to say good-bye, and asks if I've made my will.

'Going to the desert, how lovely,' she goes on. 'You'll be able to eat dates.'

'I'm hoping to have them,' I say, still smarting over Leo's lecture.

Tuesday 18 June

Leave Gloucestershire. The first irises and roses are coming out. Bands of mist lie across the foaming waves of cow parsley. It's so green and lush, I can hardly bear to tear myself away. Suffering from extreme trip-idation.

Cheer up the moment I get to Gatwick and find Patrick, the models, and three of the beards have arrived. The models are causing absolute havoc. All you can hear is the clashing of trolleys as bemused businessmen, cricking their necks for a third and fourth glance, cannon into each other. Aysha, the brunette with Charles II hair, is wearing an orange track-suit and says she has an awful tummy-ache.

Any worries about my excess baggage are banished when I see the pyramid of suitcases, wardrobe trunks, camera bags, tripods and make-up boxes labelled *The Earl of Lichfield*. Patrick, who has a passport longer than *Gone With The Wind*, and who is brilliant at putting people at their ease, further comforts me by telling me that when the King of Saudi Arabia spent the weekend with Reagan recently, he took an extra jumbo jet to carry all his luggage.

Delighted to identify one of the beards in the departure lounge as Clayton Howard, the make-up man. Having made up Princess Anne, and taught Princess Diana how flattering blue mascara is, his one unfulfilled ambition, he says, is to pluck the Queen's eyebrows. He has a goatee beard, snake-hips and the face of a reformed Mephistopheles. Gloriously camp, he manages to tell me about the horrors of eating sheeps' eyeballs on the Kenya Calendar shoot, while simultaneously exchanging laser-beam eye-meets with a handsome steward. Patrick says that when Clayton was making up the models in

Kenya, some Masai were so knocked out by his body make-up that they seriously tried to buy him.

Further delighted on the flight to identify two more beards: Chalky Whyte and Peter Kain, called Pedro by everybody – Patrick's two assistants, who have worked for him for thirteen and fourteen years respectively. Chalky, who used to play rugger for Norfolk, has light blue eyes and the sardonic street-bright face of a grown-up Artful Dodger. Pedro looks like the disciple whom Jesus loved, and radiates dependability. They are playing Scrabble with Gloria. Like a yellow Labrador puppy, her Walkman still blaring, Paula has fallen into the deep untroubled sleep of the innocent. Aysha's tummy-ache has got worse.

Ten hours later, as we fly over pale pink rocks and a vast undusted landscape, Patrick points out Las Vegas 'where all the visiting business-men go to bed early because they're so terrified of getting Aids'.

Arrive at LA. Weather in the nineties. After Arctic conditions in England, feel as though I've been locked in the sauna.

'Rather like Hampton Court maze,' I mutter as we weave our way down endless passages.

'Not as pretty,' says Patrick with a shudder.

The models cause their usual havoc. Our black porter, who has a basket-weave band on his peaked cap because it's cooler, asks Gloria to marry him. The Customs man takes one look at the curvy Aysha and bears her off to a side room for a twenty-minute frisking. Getting out of the airport seems to take more time than the flight.

'Oh my gard,' screeches a crone gliding up in a limousine longer than the QE2, 'there's the Count of Lichfield!'

We are met by Unipart's wonderfully genial public relations manager, Patrick Fitz-Gibbon.

It is now one o'clock in the morning, English time. Then follows the worst part of the journey, getting out of LA in the rush hour. Having just finished Jackie Collins's blockbuster, I am sure the jam is caused by thousands of Hollywood Wives with streaked hair from the shower, hurtling home to put their husbands' dinner in the microwave after an afternoon of adultery.

Cheered up by the mists of plumbago and agapanthus growing like bluebells along the verges. Also kept awake by Patrick Fitz-Gib-

Patrick's assistants:
Left: Chalky Whyte
Right: Peter Kain

bon's find of funny stories. Once when he was taking an American lady over an Oxford College, she turned to him, saying, 'You British are so lucky, your history is so old.' Finally reach our first-night destination, a place called Barstow, where we find Jackie, the raven-haired stylist, Alan Butler, who is the Unipart brand group manager come to keep an eye on us, and the fourth and fifth beards. Nearly fall asleep over supper. It is now 8 a.m., English time.

Good-looking American chauffeur called Romeo (pronounced as with Alfa) and I spend a long time trying to force open my bedroom door, until agitated squawking from within tells us we are on the wrong floor.

Wednesday 19 June

We all meet for breakfast. Finally identify last two beards. They are Noel Myers, the art director, who wears red glasses, looks like a rotund Windsor Davies, and has wonderful brown muscular legs that would look well on a gladiator; and Sebastian Keep – known as Keep-the-show-on-the-road. As location manager, he has the unenviable task of getting all our mountains of luggage through Customs, booking us into hotels, getting Patrick permission to photograph models, and a hundred other things. Blond and handsome, with very white teeth and a taut elegant body, he looks as Hemingway would like to have done, but is sadly out of bounds, having been married very happily for ten years to Jackie the stylist.

It was Noel and Sebastian who earlier this month spent £7,000 recce-ing Mexico, and then rang up Unipart to say they felt America, and Death Valley in particular, would be better.

'What did Unipart say?' I ask in awe.

'They said go ahead,' says Sebastian, 'they're those kind of clients.'

Outside, a hot wind blows like a hair-dryer about to fuse. It will get much worse as we near Death Valley. We are staying at the Furnace Creek Hotel, which doesn't sound promising, but if Shadrach, Meshach and Abednego could hack it, who am I to grumble?

Normality is slightly restored by Patrick ringing his London office. Percy the chauffeur would like a word, says Patrick's secretary. 'We've won the Test Match, m'lord,' says Percy. Set off for Death Valley. Patrick, Sebastian

and Noel travel in front in a hired car called the Country Squire, which gives an inappropriately suburban chime when the driver's door opens. The rest of us pile into a large van called a Winnebago. Not unlike a Weybridge den, it has pleated brown Dralon curtains, blue wallpaper, two revolving executive chairs, bench seating for ten, a loo, a fridge, and endless wardrobes. The only things missing are the copies of *Playboy* and the glasses with hunting scenes.

Pedro drives. The models take it in turns to sit beside him in front so the cold blast of the air-conditioner shoots straight up their skirts – like Marilyn Monroe in *The Seven-Year Itch*. The Carpenters are giving their all on the stereo. The models snap their fingers and sway. Clayton, the make-up man, an ex-dancer, bops up and down the corridor. Chalky, whose role on this trip is to take black and white photographs for the book and the back of the Calendar, snaps away. 'Mind the merchandise,' he says, as blonde Paula, getting a drink of water, crashes into the wardrobe.

Everyone is desperately conscious of not injuring the smooth perfection of the models' bodies. Despite Clayton's genius as a make-up man, he cannot altogether disguise bruises, and a horse-fly bite can cost £150 to touch out on a transparency. On one occasion, the entire crew waited three hours in Kenya for the perfect shot of flamingoes flying across the setting sun, only to find the model who'd been sitting on a wickerwork chair had a criss-cross bum. Clayton is extremely equable, but he did blow his top in Bali when he'd spent three hours making up a girl's face, and Patrick decided to photograph her bum instead.

As the country grows more and more like the surface of the moon, the trees get smaller and smaller. Dust devils swirl and dance, the arid plain shimmers with heat haze, flanked by mountain ranges as flat as a cardboard handkerchief in a breast pocket. The rock formations grow stranger, rearing up banana-yellow, raspberry-pink, lichen-green, like some vast WI pudding competition.

Nervously I study leaflets on Death Valley. They are full of drawings of skeletons in cars or walking across the desert. Never leave your car, they warn ominously; always tell people where you are going; always take enough water for

Twenty Mule Train Canyon – five asses look at the map.

yourself and your car, as you won't survive outside in the midday sun for more than three hours. Watch out for rattlesnakes and sidewinders, especially beneath vegetation. *Look before you step.*

Both the Winnebago and the Country Squire are armed to the teeth with walkie-talkies in case we lose each other. My nerves are not improved by finding places on the map called Funeral Mountains, Badwater, and Starvation Canyon.

The hottest, driest desert in America, Death Valley was immortalized in 1849 when a party of 'forty-niners thought they'd take a short cut west to the Californian goldfields, only to find that the snow-capped peaks that beckoned them were not the Sierras but a vast chain of uncharted mountains. Some of the party struggled on to the north-west, but a slower moving group of families made the near-fatal decision to follow the short-cut map. From here they went south across the salt flats, lost their way, and spent twenty-six days camped in the valley, burning their wagons to cook their oxen in order to survive. Eventually help came, but as they climbed out of the valley, one of the party looked back and said: 'Good-bye Death Valley.'

We are now driving past various military establishments. 'The Army, the Navy, and the Air Force all round us,' sighs Clayton, rolling his dark brown eyes in ecstasy. 'Could one ask for more?' Shut my mouth firmly so as not to breathe in the fallout. As we enter Death Valley, a huge 'DV' is carved out of the hillside, and we wonder how many of us will be coming out.

To everyone's passionate relief, the Furnace Creek Hotel is highly civilized. An oasis kept green by endless sprinklers and dotted with palms and tamarisk trees shaking their lovely fringed branches, it has a swimming pool, tennis court, air-conditioned bedrooms, two dining-rooms, a post office, and a honeymoon couple who have actually put a sticker saying 'I love being married' on their bedroom door.

Waiting for us are a film crew of four, who are making a video of the Calendar shoot for the fourth year running. Relations in the past between Lichfield's mob and the film crew have been strained. Jackie and Clayton peer out of the Winnebago to have a look.
'Gosh, *he's* put on weight, and so has *he*,' they say.

'What about that one?' I ask admiringly.

'Oh, all right,' says Jackie dismissively, 'but a bit C-O-M-M-O-N. Hi darling!' she shrieks enthusiastically as they come within earshot.

Oh God, two of the film crew have moustaches shaped like goal-posts and one has a beard — we'll be fielding a seven-a-side beard team soon.

One of the goal-post moustaches, who wears tennis whites and is as bronzed and fit as a Forest Hills champion, turns out to be Clive Davidson, the producer and director of the video and nicknamed 'the Lothario from Leigh-on-Sea' by Patrick. Clayton, however, is eyeing the youngest of the four who is clean-shaven and wears an earring. 'Girls,' he murmurs, 'I'm seriously in love again.'

The video is to be called *The Big Heat*, very appropriately, for the heat here at noon is quite appalling. I know now how frozen chickens feel when they're shoved into the microwave. It is so punishing outside that we drive the 150 yards to the restaurant, to take advantage of the air-conditioning.

After lunch, work proper starts. Patrick, as strung up as Nijinsky in the starting-gates, is champing for the off. The afternoon will be spent going through the clothes that Jackie has hired for the models. At five, the film crew want to shoot Patrick, me, and the models in a car driving along Twenty Mule Train Canyon, and at sunset there will be a dress rehearsal at Zabriskie Point.

In Jackie's room, all is chaos. The theme of the shoot, she explains, is 'the noble savage'. The clothes, which come from Western Union in LA who have provided the costumes for every cowboy movie since John Ford was a boy, will be a mixture of Red Indian, cowboy and Wild West ethnic. The models are to appear as a tribe of fierce independent Amazons who roam through the desert wearing what they can scavenge.

It's rather like the changing room at Miss Selfridge, as naked models whisk about trying on fringed suede waistcoats, fur tunics, and leather loin-cloths. The bed is littered with feathers, water bottles, head bands, knives and tomahawks.

Noel the art director watches for a few minutes, his red spectacles steaming up, and then goes and gets Patrick. It is obvious they are

We enter Death Valley – how many of us will be coming out?

far from happy. The Earl's long fingers drum on the table. Noel frantically massages his face with one hand, always a sign that all is not well.

They don't like the colours of the clothes, they say finally. The terracottas, sands, and pale greys are far too close to the rocks of Death Valley, and the girls won't show up. Patrick is also allergic to any trace of kitsch.

'I don't like that sheriff's badge on that waistcoat,' he snaps.

'It's *Annie Get Your Gun*,' protests Jackie.

'I don't care, it's awful.'

Paula emerges, unbelievably sexy in ginger suede chaps that leave her bottom and bush exposed. 'You'll be OK in that with a fanny cover,' Jackie tells her.

Gloria clinches her tiny waist with a huge leather belt. Aysha, complaining that her tummy-ache is even worse, emerges hung with leopards' tails and feathers, and wearing a black leather cap on the back of her head.

'Take it off,' says Patrick, 'it's ghastly, and it absolutely smacks of dope.'

'Patrick,' says Jackie patiently, 'these are girls who go round the desert pinching things. She's just knocked a Hell's Angel off his bike and nicked his hat.'

Clayton, oblivious of the storm breaking over his head, is trying on a fringed suede skirt.

'The colours are too near the landscape,' intones Noel.

'Then you'll have to photograph close up,' says Jackie.

'I'm not going to,' says Patrick coldly. 'The trouble with most girly calendars is you see far too much girl. Why can't they wear white?'

'White looks like an Omo ad.'

'If we have girls wearing the same colours as the countryside they'll get lost,' says Patrick. 'The thinking's not big enough. Fiona only stood out in Bali last year because she wore orange. The landscape's so fantastic here, the girls have really got to zing.'

'They *will* zing,' protests Jackie. 'Imagine a girl by a boulder in this amazing gear, with strange make-up, like a kid dropped out from LA.'

'A total nude against those cliffs would really blow their minds,' says Noel excitedly.

'If you show nudes,' points out Sebastian, who has just arrived to provide the voice of reason, 'we'll be in trouble with the Ranger.' Clayton is now trying on a bone necklace and a pair of dinosaur's teeth earrings.

'The less dressed they are the better,' says Patrick firmly.

'I got a briefing that nudity wasn't essential,' snaps Jackie.

'As the girls get smaller, they can get nuder.'

'I want them to look wild and strange,' wails Jackie.

Noel shakes his grey head. 'They'll be too small to look anything.'

'And, old bean,' says Patrick, the husky, infinitely sexy smoker's voice taking on a bitchy upper-class ring, 'they won't show up in those skin tones.'

There is plainly a conflict of interests.

On to Twenty Mule Train Canyon, through which in the last century the mule-teams used to drag the newly mined borax out of Death Valley. Here the film crew shoot us hurtling along looking animated, as Patrick drives the Country Squire like Niki Lauda. The rocks, rising all round us to a gentian-blue sky, stop the heartbeat. It is as though we have been pitched into Brobdignag, where the cook has gone to bed drunk, leaving huge gold loaves, haphazardly baked in a hundred different shapes, and vast tawny pease puddings moulded with pudgy fingers, littered around the kitchen. Further down the Canyon, the giant's children have been building massive sandcastles, and perhaps burying their father – any second you expect to see ten-foot toes sticking out of the sand.

On to Zabriskie Point, which is even more staggering. Yellow, brown and grey rocks lie beneath us like the backs of animals – lion, hippo, rhino – trapped as they stampede through a narrow canyon. To the left is the Badlands Ridge, capped by antimacassars of black lava from earthquakes five million years ago. On the right is Manly Beacon, named after the heroic William Manly who led the ill-fated 'forty-niners out of Death Valley.

Zabriskie Point, named according to the guidebook, after 'an early-day executive of the borax mining company,' rears up: a perfect equilateral triangle. In the distance the salt flats gleam like snow.

This is to be the site of the first shoot at sunrise tomorrow. Aware of Patrick's disapproval, the

Zabriskie Point

models have lost much of their brio. Paula, in a black fur tunic and one black fur garter, her face and thighs daubed with war paint, poses on a smooth grey dome waving a scaly black whip unpleasantly reminiscent of a rattlesnake. She looks neither noble nor savage.

'That dress won't do,' says Patrick. 'It's rabbit.'

Chalky takes black and white pictures. Pedro rushes round with a compass and light-meter looking at angles, trying to work out exactly where the sun will rise tomorrow. Aysha rolls up looking as though she's been to a jumble sale, a Midi Maha dwarfed by a long black skirt, a waistcoat, and once again the black peaked cap.

'Take it *off!*' explodes Patrick. 'She looks like a German bus conductor.'

Delighted by such friction, the film crew whisk about filming everything.

Gloria in a grey suede waistcoat and white baseball trousers, who can never look anything other than exquisite, picks her way over some very dangerous rocks and takes up her position on the back of one of the trapped lions. Patrick and Noel have a shouting match about her clothes. Isolated by the burning wind, she cannot hear Patrick's instructions to 'Relax, stand at ease, no do the bloody thing you were doing before that, no before bloody that, darling! For Christ's sake relax.'

'I am relaxing!' she screams back.

Confused, blown like a grey leaf by their arguments and tension, she decides to sit down.

'No, for Christ's sake get up, darling.' Patrick's voice is steel-tipped with irritation.

I feel faint and go and sit in the Winnebago. So desperate with thirst, find I have drunk half a cup of water intended for the radiator.

Later I watch them coming down the winding mountain path, silhouetted against the setting sun. The Unipart brand group manager, Alan Butler, and Patrick Fitz-Gibbon carry Gloria who has a blister. Paula strides ahead like a young Amazon. Clayton, who has moulded one of the white pudding-basin sun hats provided by Unipart into a trilby, puffs on his long cigarette-holder and holds a red, white and blue umbrella over Aysha. Then come Pedro and Chalky humping camera equipment, and finally Patrick and Noel, both their arms waving as they shout at one another.

Jackie is amazingly calm. I would be suicidal at such a lack of enthusiasm. She explains that her mother was a casting director at the BBC and her father, Gordon Cryer, produced and wrote 'ITMA' and 'Band Wagon' and most of Emile Littler's pantomimes. Having spent her childhood snatching sleep in dressing-rooms backstage or on film locations, she is unfazed by histrionics and tantrums.

'It's just first-night nerves,' she says. 'It happens every year. Try and put the clothes back on the hangers, girls.'

'We've done eight calendars, and it's always like this,' says Clayton, putting the top back on a blue lipstick. 'Last year,' he goes on with a gentle smile on his face, 'Patrick sat on a scorpion and it drew blue blood.'

'Last year he had 187 mosquito bites,' adds Jackie with a carrion-crow screech of laughter.

Back at the Furnace Creek Hotel, I discover a book called *Death Valley Victims* in the gift shop, which lists all the people who've died here, most of them from heat exposure or snake bites. Am alarmed to find a Cooper in the index, but find he only buried some victim called Eichbum.

On the way to bed, kind Clayton sidles up to me and says to be sure to block up the plug-holes of the wash basin and the bath, and to put the loo seat down, in case I am invaded by scorpions, tarantulas or rattlesnakes. Spend the rest of the night listening to the roar of the air-conditioning, and suffering from rattle fatigue.

Thursday 20 June

Up at four to shoot at Zabriskie Point. As the sun rises, Paula, wearing rust suede trousers, a gold waistcoat and a grey Confederate States peaked cap, stands on a yellow fold of giant's doll's-house Yorkshire pudding. It is blissfully cool now – about 100 degrees. Patrick, a coronet on his blue shirt, white Unipart shorts emphasizing the long racehorse legs, is looking at a Polaroid with Noel, discussing whether they want to change the cropping of the picture. Clayton, braving rattlesnakes and spiders, hides behind a rock.

'OK, more dramatic, darling,' shouts Patrick, starting to shoot. The landscape seems to strut and pose. Patrick turns to Jackie: 'Do you think she should have less on?'

'We can't do nudes, we haven't got permis-

Clayton puts Aysha in the shade.

sion from the Ranger,' says Sebastian, making an off drive with a Unipart umbrella.

Patrick ignores him. 'Take off your top, darling.' Clayton in his white trilby darts out from behind the rock and starts peeling garments off Paula. As she leans forward, shielding her eyes with her hand, thrusting out her breasts, the rising sun touches her rouged nipples. 'It's the Frontier Look,' says Jackie triumphantly.

'Can't get much frontier than that,' says Noel, mopping his brow.

'Shut up,' says Jackie, 'or I'll put ice down your shorts.'

Now Paula is naked except for a G-string and the peaked cap, the sun turning her rosy-brown.

Patrick: 'God, this is good, drop your left shoulder slightly, darling, Noel this is sensational.'

Noel (over the walkie-talkie): 'Dramatize the neck a bit, darling.'

Paula lifts her head; Patrick clicks away frenziedly, Pedro keeping him supplied with

'That'll do,' says Patrick, taking a last Polaroid, 'that's just the sort of shot I want, Jackie.'

'Well I'm going home then,' snaps Jackie.

Aysha arrives for the next shot, complaining of headache as well as tummy-ache. Hung with leopards' tails and feathers, she looks like an advertisement for *Fur and Feather*. We then have the absurd spectacle of her and Clayton tripping over the rocks together, Clayton shielding her with an umbrella like Little Black Sambo.

Having broken his duck, Patrick perks up enough to tell us that when he filled his swimming pool in Mustique recently, it was as expensive as filling it with Perrier, such is the cost of water in that part of the world.

At that moment Paula comes bounding up wearing nothing but a Unipart T-shirt. 'I've just seen the most beautiful snake,' she cries. 'Two feet long, and all rainbow coloured. I tried to catch him, but he was too quick.' Feeling Paula and I have slightly different attitudes to wildlife, I nervously tighten the laces of my Kickers.

Aysha and Clayton have now reached the top of the peak. 'They need crampons,' said Paula. 'Isn't that a dead rude word?'

Noel bounds up the rock like a mountain goat to explain to Aysha how she should pose, and then bounds back again.

'It's very steep on the other side of that rock,' he says as Aysha sways unnervingly. Clayton skips behind another boulder.

'Look mean, darling,' says Patrick gazing into the camera.

'Put those rats' tails between your tits and point, darling,' screams Jackie over the walkie-talkie.

As the sun rises and shadows shrink, the scrub on the rocks looks like bleached hedgehogs. Pedro keeps Patrick constantly supplied with light readings, as everything sharpens up.

Patrick: 'Get out of the way, Clayton, we've really got to steam now, the light's starting to bleach out.'

Aysha, down to her cowboy boots now, bum cleavage echoed by the cleavage of the rocks, is pointing into the middle distance. But just as we are getting the perfect shot, a car draws up. Terrified it might be the Ranger, Jackie bellows to Aysha to cover herself up. There is no time for her to get back into her skirt and waistcoat. Gallantly Clayton whips off his T-shirt, and tugs it over her head. 'I've never been topless before,' he grumbles.

'Don't worry,' shouts Jackie, 'we'll adjust your fee.'

Then we all pretend frantically to be sightseeing and studying rock formations. But the car turns out not to be the Ranger but, almost worse, a couple with two small children who peel themselves stickily off the seats of their car like Polaroids, and spend ten minutes locating the various beauty spots. Sweat darkens our T-shirts and courses down our bodies; precious shadows drain away as we wait, and wait.

At last they drive away.

'Get your gear off, darling,' yells Patrick, 'hide Clayton, look at the light on that bum.'

Legs apart, Aysha is totally naked now, Medusa curls descending in an inky waterfall. 'It's a bit fashiony, darling, do what you feel happy with, but keep it strong,' says Jackie. Aysha stretches out her arms and her shadow falls like an X-certificate across the yellow rock. The perfect pose. Last roll – and it's a wrap.

Patrick mops his brow, you can almost see the tension draining out of him. 'Christ, I feel like Icarus about to melt. The problem is to produce

Oh what a lovely squaw!

a picture that isn't going to be boring for a whole calendar month.'

Back in the Winnebago, the girls are wandering about naked. Bums and bushes pass at eye-level as they get dressed. They look so gorgeous that I cannot think why the crew don't rush in and ravish them, but they seem as unmoved as window-dressers putting clothes on a polystyrene model in a Harrods window. 'In fact,' explains Chalky, 'one somehow finds models far more attractive in the evening when they've got their clothes on.'

Revelling in first-shoot euphoria, we bop back to the hotel in raging spirits, singing 'There must be a letter today, Mr Postman.' Noel gazes at Paula: 'I do like girls in men's shirts, they look so vulnerable,' he says wistfully.

'I prefer the real thing,' says Clayton crisply, zipping up a case containing hundreds of coloured pencils.

'When are we going to have our first barbecue?' asks Jackie.

'Just chuck a steak on the pavement and it'll cook,' says Clayton.

By the time we get back to breakfast it is nine o'clock and 115 degrees. Frantic with thirst, we fall on vats of orange juice, and eggs and bacon, desperate to replace all the salt we have sweated away. Also on the menu are date bread, sheet cake and dry sand. The butter is piled high in shampoo sachets in a slot machine. '*Please take butter from the bottom*,' says a large sign.

Afterwards we leap into the swimming pool. I get there early, so I can hide under the blue water. Wish I'd stuck to my crash diet. Poor Aysha has retired to bed with her aches, but Paula and Gloria play tag and water polo with Noel, Sebastian and the camera crew. There is a lot of slap and tickle. Clayton enters the pool cautiously and swims up and down the shallow end, his head held high out of the water like a housewife protecting her beehive.

The pool attendant, who has grey hair like a faded chrysanthemum spiking out from a dark-blue cap, and who looks too spaced out to attend to anything, offers a dollar to anyone who can guess the temperature. It is 122 degrees. The handrails on the steps into the pool are like molten lead; no one dares be exposed to the sun for more than five minutes.

Clive Davidson, the Lothario from Leigh-on-Sea, arrives smiling, watchful, and vulpine. He is certainly in great shape, with his flashing mahogany legs and his flat stomach. But there is plainly no love lost between him and the Earl. Perhaps there is an element of sexual jealousy, both in their own very different circles used to effortlessly attracting women.

The first year that they made a film of the Calendar shoot, Patrick let down the tyres of Clive's Porsche. Another year, the camera crew tried to throw Clive fully clothed into the pool. Yet another year, Clayton made up Patrick and Noel with black eyes and terrible bruises. When the film crew rolled up, everyone pretended they had just had a terrible fight. The excitement with which the film crew started to shoot turned to rage when Noel suddenly rubbed his eye and all the black and purple smudged.

Obviously with a few scores to settle, Clive is hell-bent on stirring up trouble this year in order to make *The Big Heat* a more exciting film. He tells me all the models are miserable and fed up with being treated badly. Shrieks of merriment from the pool belie this. Even worse, from now on he wants me to be miked up all the time that Patrick is shooting so I can make scintillating comments.

Despite the fact that his team are all at times victims of his feudal caprice, the Earl certainly inspires devotion in them. He won't allow any insubordination. Only this morning he bawled Noel out for offering a wilting model a beer before breakfast. He is irascible, with an extremely short fuse, and as a result he frequently upsets people; but he is so mortified afterwards they always forgive him – not least, too, because he has more charm than anyone I have ever met. A beauty in his youth, he has grown far more attractive in middle age, with the grey tumbleweed hair, the shrewd fox-brown eyes, and the craggy battered Western-hero features which are suddenly transformed by a wicked schoolboy grin.

At lunch, elated by his first morning's shooting, he is in coruscating form. It is rather like listening to a dazzling after-dinner speech, as one hilarious, scurrilous anecdote follows another. How he photographed Dean Martin and even the dog was drunk. How he was sent to photograph a famous Hollywood movie star's wife, who turned out to be a very butch army

Left: The Lothario from Leigh-on-Sea
Right: Patrick

colonel. Now he is regaling us with a story about David Bailey trying to photograph eleven lords a-leaping for a Christmas colour magazine issue. Having gathered eight peers and three bishops in his studio, Bailey forgot himself enough to shout, 'Now jump, you fuckers!' whereupon the senior bishop turned as purple as his raiment, flounced out, and Bailey was left with ten lords and no shot.

We shoot again at sunset. Clayton is making up Gloria, turning her into a little Apache. 'Madame has a great face with nice far-apart eyes,' he sighs, 'but it leaks. I always think "leaks" sounds so much nicer than "sweats". The light deepens at sunrise and sunset, so I'm applying a terracotta shadow called Rich Bitch to her eyes.' Now he's putting on war-paint, blue and yellow on the cheeks, red down the forehead, and black on the nose.

Gloria started modelling, she says, as soon as she left college. She looked up all the clothing manufacturers in the Yellow Pages, then rang them, asking if they needed a showroom model, and after a lot of pestering she got a job. Aysha lies on the bed and says she was working in Underwoods, selling Estée Lauder, when a 'lady came in, said I was pretty, and gave me the name of an agent. At first they wouldn't look at me, they said I was too little.'

Both girls complain of the expense of putting together a portfolio of photographs: it can cost at least £300.

'I couldn't get any work in 1982,' says Gloria. 'I'm not girl-next-door enough. They said my portfolio was too exotic.'

'I'd like to do girl-next-door,' says Aysha wistfully, 'but they only want blondes.'

Neither of them has any urge to be a Page 3 girl in the *Sun*. 'Although it used to be prestigious in Jilly Johnson's time, it isn't any more,' says Gloria.

'You only get £50 anyway,' grumbles Aysha, tossing back her Medusa curls. 'There ought to be a models' union.'

All the time they watch themselves in the mirror, checking that they're still there. Both are saying how much they enjoy the work when Noel, spiky grey hair on end, red specs askew, comes in and collapses into an armchair, saying he isn't sure if *he* enjoys work any more, and he

finds working with both client and photographer at the same time a terrible strain. He then goes on to deflate both Gloria and Aysha by saying the life of a model is very short.

'You have to compete with seventeen-year-olds whose knockers are hitting the ceiling. After twenty-three, tits start getting droopy, and girls don't look as good.'

Gloiria, who is all of twenty-four, pulls a face at Noel and is reproved by Clayton who is trying to apply green lipstick.

Up at Zabriskie Point, the sun is sinking. Sebastian is holding an umbrella over Patrick and Noel, who are having a full-dress row over how to shoot the next picture.

I mutter that they are all behaving like children. Notice Clive the film director's eyes gleaming as he orders the sound man to mike me up. His disappointment is palpable when, on being asked what I think of the shoot so far, I stoutly reply: 'I am amazed how extraordinarily hard everyone is working, and how well they are all getting on.'

Aysha then arrives in the waistcoat and long black skirt, a necklace of mammoth's teeth nibbling her breasts. She looks like a little girl who's been at her mother's dressing-up box. Gloria, who is to be shot first, turns up in the grey fringed waistcoat, and is bollocked for forgetting her tomahawk. Sebastian is sent off down the mountain to retrieve it.

Because the sun sets very quickly in Death Valley, within half an hour, and time is so short, Patrick and Noel suspend their row and decide to shoot Aysha first. 'Go over there and do something exciting on that rock,' Patrick tells Noel irritably.

As Noel scampers over the lunar landscape like a mountain goat, then collapses on a grey plateau like a beached whale saying, 'Is this any good, Guv'nor?' I decide his relationship with Patrick is very like Falstaff's with Prince Hal.

Soon Aysha reaches the plateau under Clayton's umbrella, and is once again arranged by Noel. Patrick is just about to start shooting when we are interrupted by the arrival of three German tourists – two men with legs hairier than Pan's coming out of long Baden-Powell shorts, and their very plain girlfriend who has yachts in harbour printed all over her shirt.

'Cover up, girls,' urges Jackie, '*nous avons*

Gloria

company.' Quickly Aysha and Gloria wriggle back into their Indian gear, trying not to get war-paint on the suede, and pretend to be earnestly studying rock formations.

'You make picture for magazine?' ask the Germans.

'No, a calendar for parts,' says Chalky.

The Germans refuse to budge, despite some-one pointedly whistling 'The Dambusters', so in the end Patrick carries on shooting regardless.

'Walk towards me, darling,' he calls to Aysha. She starts to pick her way daintily across the rock. 'No one walks like that!'

'Ay do,' says Aysha petulantly.

'Get her gear off, Clayton – and do something *dramatic*, darling.' Aysha, naked now, sinks into the lotus position. The Germans puff fixedly on their Marlboros, piggy light-blue eyes out on stalks.

'Jackie,' bellows Patrick, 'her tits are purple, can't we do anything about them?'

Jackie darts forward with the Panstik.

The sun is going; the mountains, losing their colour, turn from gold to dull red-brown.

'Don't you get nervous taking your clothes off in front of all these people?' I ask Gloria and Paula.

They look amazed and say, not at all. They are proud of their bodies and feel much happier and less self-conscious without clothes, although they resent outsiders like the Germans gawping.

Aysha is lying on her back now, naked except for her G-string, the picture of abandonment. The German girl, the yachts on her large bosom rising and falling in disapproval, is furiously photograhing Zabriskie Point. Her companions are unashamedly photographing Aysha's finer points. Patrick is shooting the last roll.

'Lovely, darling, but I can see your pubes.'

Aysha adjusts her G-string – and it's a wrap. As the light has gone, there is no time to shoot Gloria. The camera bags are zipped up to keep out the heat and dust. They are, Patrick tells me, copies of US medical orderly first-aid bags, which were adopted by some of the *Life* maga-zine photographers assigned to the Vietnam War.

Back at the hotel, feeling impossibly hot and sweaty, we go straight into dinner. The Ameri-cans are certainly into Cuisine Grosseur. Every plate is piled high with chips, shredded lettuce, and massive steaks. Most of us share one steak between two, but still can't begin to finish up. Patrick orders some red wine, which is tepid, unbelievably disgusting, and will certainly strip off the inside of our throats. 'There are too few chefs and not enough Indians in this country,' he says, smothering his steak with Lea and Perrins.

Gloria, who couldn't bother to change, is wearing a black and white dressing gown. With her tits falling out, her war-paint smudged on her face, she looks unbelievably touching – like Eliza Doolittle. Already the beards and the film crew are beginning to step around the models. Everyone is watching everyone else like hawks, looking for (in Patrick's words) 'evidence of a leg-over situation'. It seems, however, that both Gloria and Aysha are bespoke. Gloria is getting married to an interior decorator of forty-one at the end of July. He is absolutely awesome, she says, her huge eyes gleaming. Aysha, who still has a tummy-ache and a headache, says she has a fiancé called Brett le Stafford, who is in videos. 'He thinks the world of me,' she goes on. 'He's already rung me nine times today. Being in videos, he's never at a loss, he keeps my Nan in stitches.'

Paula, the ravishing blonde, seems to be the only one available, but proceeds to dash every-one's hopes by announcing her boyfriend is a Venezuelan tycoon with 'a dick that big' – wickedly she holds her sun-tanned hands a yard apart. The wolves retreat, daunted. 'There's a serious lack of available crumpet on this trip,' says Chalky in disgust.

Patrick, who hasn't been listening, turns to Gloria. 'I hear you're marrying some boring engineer,' he says. He then proceeds to tell the story of a model who came out to South Carolina on a Calendar trip some years ago and on the first day's shooting, wrapped in lace, announced that she didn't do nudes because her boyfriend disapproved. Pandemonium broke out, and she was nearly sent back. After a shouting match with her agents, they contacted her boyfriend and asked if he was prepared to foot the bill for the return air-fare of another model? 'Within minutes the clothes came off.'

'I don't think she put them on for the rest of the trip,' said Chalky.

It is now midnight; realize we have been on the march since four.

The Americans are definitely into *cuisine grosseur* – so, it seems, are the British.

Long to wear shorts like everyone else, but too ashamed of my pale legs. Decide to put on fake tan, but too much *in vino* to smooth it on properly.

Friday 21 June

Up four hours later to shoot at Dante's View. Find that I have dark-orange heels and toes, white ankles, and calves striped orange like a tiger. Cover the whole thing up with trousers once more.

I travel in the Country Squire with Sebastian and Patrick. Even the most minor roads in America are like a major road between Oxford and Swindon. As we drive up and up, the scrub becomes more luxuriant. One plant even has tiny scarlet flowers. The light is scabious-blue as the sun rises; the mountains are dark-red, as though someone has dripped claret over them.

'They look like summer puddings,' I say.

'Midsummer puddings,' says Patrick. 'It's the longest day. The main problem in this heat,' he goes on, 'is flat nipples,' and he launches into a yarn about one of his corporals who refused promotion because he had a better job awaiting him in Civvy Street, putting ice on showgirls' nipples at the Windmill.

A jack-rabbit lopes across our paths. The view at the top is staggering. Five thousand feet below us the salt flats gleam incandescent, unearthly, as though the snow has crept down from the peaks and stretched out in the valley to sunbathe. Opposite, vast strawberry-roan mountains surge up to a cranesbill-blue sky. 'Awesome,' murmurs Sebastian, brushing his blond hair out of his eyes, 'parsitively awesome.'

I ponder which sinners in Dante's *Inferno* would be punished by being left continually raging with thirst in the burning salt. Probably the heavy drinkers. At the rate I have been knocking back the vodka, I shall certainly qualify. Although, being dehydrated, it takes about one stiff drink to lay you out in this temperature.

According to the guidebook, which always seems to ruin any romance, we are looking down on 'a salt-chemical desert, and in a few days any living thing out there would be embalmed like salt cod, preserved forever, and thoroughly dead'.

Feel utterly repulsive this morning. My white ankles have already swelled up like duffle bags, my face is like a baron of beef from yesterday's sun. As a result of wearing a belt with a metal buckle to carry the film crew's microphone yesterday, I have developed a metal allergy and am raging with prickly heat. Seek refuge in the Winnebago, where Gloria, looking stunning with everything – nose, eyes, curls, tits, bum – tip-tilted, is wandering around naked. As Jackie dresses her in a brown squaw's jerkin, Jackie and I start quoting *Hiawatha* line by line at one another.

'Oh, I'd give anything in the world to have brains like you two,' says Gloria sadly.

We look at her incredulously. 'But we'd give anything to have a body like yours,' Jackie and I chorus.

Then we all laugh and feel better, and much less inadequate.

Outside, the light has lost its purple tinge; the shadow that was half-way up the mountain when we arrived now lies half-way across the salt flats. Jackie has put one baseball pad on Gloria's left thigh.

'Take it off,' says Patrick predictably, the moment he sees her.

Now she is posing on a very precarious rocky mound, with Clayton hovering behind among the creosote bushes to catch her if she falls off. She goes into a sequence of marvellously natural poses, fierce, vulnerable, proud. Now she is pretending to shoot a bow and arrow. Gradually her clothes are peeled off, till she is down to a G-string and a lasso over her shoulder.

A nice woman at the hotel last night told me that the rattle of a rattlesnake sounds like dry seeds being shaken in a roll of parchment. Find myself listening obsessively for the sound. Chalky tries to cheer me up. 'What sounds like a rattlesnake,' he explains, 'is Clayton abusing himself.'

'Do you think his thing's so old it's got scales on it?' says Sebastian.

Clayton giggles, blossoming in the attention like a paper flower.

'Great body,' mutters Pedro, gazing at Gloria.

'Easily the best . . .' begins Noel. Like lightning Patrick puts a warning hand on Noel's arm, Noel catches sight of Paula sitting on a nearby rock, and changes it to 'Easy on the eye.'

'One tit's higher than the other, well higher,'

Patrick, allergic to any sign of kitsch, soon had the baseball pad off.

says Jackie.

'Take off her G-string,' says Patrick.

Clayton skips round to undo it. Meanwhile the sun is rising relentlessly.

'Hurry *up*. He's obviously had no practice with this kind of thing,' says Patrick, as Clayton picks delicately away at the knot, determined not to break his nails.

Shadows groove the hills, the sun idly fingers the neighbouring mountains which are lilac now, a heliotrope haze lies over the white bleached lake.

'Duck, Clayton!' yells Patrick, excited as a schoolboy at the prospect of a mega-shot, and it's a wrap.

Paula, wearing a grey waistcoat once worn by Kris Kristofferson, is now climbing the slope of the hill. The perfect contrast to Gloria's dusky beauty, she looks like a Russian Art Deco poster, like a young Apollo climbing into the sun's rays. Next minute Clayton is whisking through the creosote bushes, tarantulas and rattlesnakes forgotten, to tweak Paula's nipples which have flattened in the heat.

'Is her hair neat and tidy?' asks Jackie, but nobody cares. Patrick, as we all do, responds to her amazing golden beauty: 'Fan-bloody-tastic.'

Off comes Kris Kristofferson's waistcoat, as she arches her body out to meet the sun and a last roll is shot. Everyone bursts into a round of applause as we surge forward to look at the Polaroids. As we pile into the Winnebago, Noel sits heavily on my straw hat.

Patrick is a workaholic. He doesn't sleep at night worrying about the next day's shoot, walking his box like a nervous horse. By day, when he is not taking pictures, he is relentlessly searching for the perfect place to shoot the next one. Why does he do it? 'If you're born an amateur, you have to try that little bit harder to prove you're a professional,' he says.

At noon we drive the Country Squire out to the salt flats on which we have just been looking down. The lowest place in the western hemisphere, 282 feet below sea-level, it is called Badwater. Noel immediately trots off to have a pee and 'makes it even worse water,' says Sebastian.

Patrick and I make silly jokes about fish swimming by and bumping into Cousteau. The salt, close up, is incredible, like the inside of a vast Bounty bar; the glaze murders the eyeballs.

'What could a model be doing?' muses Patrick. 'Throwing salt over her left shoulder?'

The light is perfect. 'Why don't we shoot now?' asks Noel.

'Because we haven't brought any crumpet, you wally,' says Patrick.

'Oh, I thought they were in the Winnebago,' says Noel. 'I seem to be losing track.'

The sun seems to be deranging us all, it is like sitting in an oven on Regulo 9. Acutely conscious of a sweating magenta face, I can think of absolutely nothing witty to say to the film crew. *I must try and be less vain.*

Everyone grumbles about the heat, until Patrick launches into a saga about an Antarctic expedition where someone's willy got frost-bite when he nipped out to have a pee, which makes everyone feel less resentful. After much bickering it is decided to shoot Paula riding a horse across the salt flats, at exactly the same time tomorrow.

We then move on to an even hotter spot called the Devil's Golf Course. Here, because it is the longest day, and true to their video title *The Big Heat*, Clive and the film crew shoot Patrick trying to fry an egg on the bonnet of the Country Squire. Despite the murderous heat, the egg white refuses to go opaque. 'Not what you'd call a fast-food restaurant,' says Sebastian.

Just when I'm nervously wondering whether I'm going to expire, and swell the addendum of the Death Valley victims, Patrick gets fed up with the lack of progress and drops another egg on the bonnet, which slithers down and disappears into the radiator. We play cricket with the rest; I drop two very easy catches. The film company, bored, go home. Shrieking, we ease ourselves back on to the burning car seats, when a terrific bang followed by massive reverberations makes us jump out of our skins.

'Nudes I can take,' grumbles Noel, 'but not nukes.'

On the way back Patrick, who went to Harrow, and Sebastian who went to Beaumont, a Catholic school, have a somewhat upmarket discussion about school rugger matches, and how Beaumont had to stop and say five Hail Marys every time they said 'Bugger' in the scrum. They then move on to prep school and

Patrick tries to fry eggs on the bonnet at noon on the longest day. Jilly, Sebastian and Noel fry anyway.

how awful it was having loos without any doors. After a minute Noel, a Cockney who missed five years of schooling because he was in London during the Blitz, asks in a puzzled voice, 'How did you get into the loos, then?'

We are still howling with mirth when we get back to the hotel, to be greeted by Paula in tears of happiness: her Venezuelan boyfriend has asked her to marry him. She says she will, when she makes her fortune.

Alan Butler, the Unipart brand group manager, is going home tomorrow. He says it will be a little difficult to settle down to strategy planning after such a lively few days away from the office. He is a very sweet man, and has worked overtime humping suitcases and camera bags, and deliberately not interfering. I wish clients had been like that when I worked in advertising. We shall all miss him.

At dinner, he buys us champagne. Noel, who has sat on and broken his red spectacles, orders trout and tells the waitress he wants it rare. 'It must be rare in this part of the world,' says Patrick.

Noel then tells me about making the Kenya Unipart Calendar. 'We went to a place', he says, his eyes shining, 'where no white man had ever been before.'

'Terrifying for the blacks,' drawls Patrick, 'seeing you as their first ever-white man.'

'How did they react?' I ask.

'They got into their Cadillacs and drove away,' said Noel.

Patrick shudders when someone passes the port the wrong way, and then, almost with tears in his eyes, tells me in an undertone how much he adores Noel. 'A sweet, sensitive, funny, amazingly talented man. I always see all the problems, Noel has gut instinct.' He goes on to explain that the blazing rows, the teasing, and the endless badinage, are all part of a formalized ritual to get the adrenalin going and produce the best pictures.

I suppose it's rather like Tweedledum saying, 'Let's fight until six, and then have dinner.' Although Patrick would never dine at such an unfashionably early hour.

Meanwhile Clive, the Lothario from Leigh-on-Sea, sits at the end of the table, watching for signs of friction. Tonight there are none, sad to relate.

Saturday morning, 22 June

We all go up to Zabriskie Point for a group shot. Clayton, a symphony in white and turquoise, checks his hair at the back with two mirrors. Patrick tells Aysha to sit down on a rock. 'I can't sit down in a frying pan,' she grumbles. In addition to headache and backache, she says, she now has cystitis.

Pedro sets up the shot and then races down the rock to join us and get in the picture.

'What day is it?' asks Paula.

'Saturday,' I tell her.

'I'd be in the King's Road shopping,' she says wistfully.

'It's now nine o'clock in the evening in England,' says Patrick.

'Then I'd be partying,' she says even more wistfully.

Suddenly one realizes how young she is – and indeed all the models are – when she reveals the fact that her mother is only thirty-seven, the same age as Chalky and Pedro, nine years younger than Patrick and eleven years younger than me.

'Give me your Mum's address, and I'll pop round and see her some time,' says Noel.

Patrick tells me how they were all brought up with a start at the end of one Calendar shoot, when a model announced that she had never dreamed people of her parents' age could be such fun.

At noon we return to Badwater with a slightly scruffy liver chestnut with furry legs like a feminist, called Snort. Unlike the rest of us mad English, Snort is not remotely put out by the midday sun. His master, who is called Dick, says Snort originally came from a herd of wild horses and doesn't like other horses but is very fond of ass. This is patently obvious. From the moment Paula, wearing nothing but a G-string, gauntlets and a cowboy hat, scrambles on to his back, Snort resolutely sticks out a long dappled cock and refuses to put it in.

Paula, who used to be a jockey, rides very well, and is soon zig-zagging Snort back and forth across the salt flats, which gleam like molten pearl. You can't see the surrounding mountains for dust. Patrick shoots from the top of the Winnebago, the temperature is 125 degrees, the glare from the salt is excruciating. Perhaps we shall all be blinded like Peeping Tom

Patrick shoots from the top of the Winnebago. Dick, Sebastian and Jackie seek the 125° shade.

for gazing on a Lady Godiva with no long hair to cover her.

Finally Snort decides to de-expose himself.

'Sensational,' says Patrick, clicking away. 'Don't let her hat blow off or we'll be chasing it all afternoon.'

Dick says that when he was first captured, Snort fought because he was scared, but now he's a model horse, pulling the plough, the mowing machine, and even a sledge in winter. 'A sledge!' I said in amazement.

'We actually had a frost last year,' said Dick proudly. 'Everyone came out to look at it.'

Just as Patrick is about to wrap, Paula puts one leg over, going into an impromptu side-saddle position so beautiful that another roll has to be shot. One often finds models fall instinctively into the pose that will make the best picture. I am constantly amazed at how patient and long-suffering they are, endangering their lives as they pose for hours on high rocks or in the burning sun. This trio give themselves no airs in a G-string.

Driving home we see a car parked on the side of the road, surrounded by a group of people. One of the locals, unable to cope with Death Valley any more, has blown his brains out.

Cheer up over lunch, when Patrick, who has been on the telephone to England, tells us an employee has been sacked from Selfridges for feeding a blue film into the closed-circuit television sets around the store.

Discussion moves on to a tart in London who was paid £75,000 for four minutes by some Arab.

'Gosh, I'd be tempted,' I say to Sebastian. 'Would you let Jackie?'

Sebastian looks thoughtful. 'I think I'd let Jackie do it for ten minutes,' he says.

Poor Aysha is obviously beginning to feel excluded. Every day she produces a new symptom, perhaps to draw attention to herself. She is a very beautiful girl, but – gentle, romantic-looking, utterly feminine – she is totally miscast as a proud, tough savage fending for herself in the desert; whereas Paula and Gloria fall naturally into the role – and as a result are being used much more.

Tonight Aysha lounges on the bed, a symbol of disgruntlement, watching Clayton make up Gloria yet again for a shot at sunset. 'I'm so hungry,' she grumbles, 'and so tired.' Her boyfriend has rung her nine times again today to say how much he's missing her. He gets up every morning at home, she goes on, and brings her toast and a vitamin tablet in bed.

No one takes much notice; Jackie and Clayton are dressing Gloria, teasing her black curls above her beaded headdress, putting Blue-Tak on her nipples to stiffen them. The thing models hate most, explains Gloria kindly, is being on a trip and not being used.

'Brett's rung me nine times today,' Aysha tells us again. 'He says "I miss you so much," and my Mum's rung me, she says she's missing me too.'

One has a feeling, poor child, she would forgo all these telephone calls for an opportunity to stand on the rock in the burning heat tonight and endure a taste of Patrick's bullying. She reminds me of Margot Asquith: 'If you have been sunned through and through like an apricot on a wall from your earliest days, you are over-sensitive to any withdrawal of heat.'

The days seem to be gliding into one another. Groups constantly form and re-form, getting close like starlings at dusk. People suddenly feel excluded as new friendships are struck up, or one person gets more attention at dinner, or one end of the table at meal-times is more rowdy and riotous than the other. Cabals form in rooms, chatting, dissecting: 'he said,' 'she said,' 'he said,' 'he didn't?' 'the bastard, the *absolute* bastard!' Not for nothing in Death Valley is one of the largest mountains called the Grapevine.

All of us, I suppose, have our own vested interests. Patrick wants to take the best pictures. The models want to appear as beautiful and as often as possible. Jackie and Clayton want them to look beautiful in her clothes and his make-up. I am desperate to write a good book. The film company are equally desperate to make a good video of *The Big Heat*.

I am absorbing copy all the time like a sponge, but find it impossibly difficult to squeeze the sponge and come out with brilliant one-liners for the video. I know the film company are disappointed by my lack of co-operation.

We are all – thank goodness – gradually coming to terms with the heat. The sun is like a guard dog; it now allows us to pat it gingerly, but one does not take liberties. One of the magic

Snort arrives at the salt flats.

Paula and Gloria —
two ravishing fillies
admire other fillies.

things, too, about Death Valley is that the air is so dry that when one washes one's hair the hot winds outside blow-dry it absolutely straight and smooth, and one has none of the normal hassle about fitting hair-dryers into plugs.

Jackie produces numerous games to keep us amused during the day, when it is too hot to shoot. One of them is called 'I am a Famous Person' in which one has to pretend to be any celebrity, from Boy George to Henry VIII to Lucretia Borgia, and others have to guess who the person is.

On Sunday we have a swimming relay race. Having spent so much time on location abroad, most of the group swim extremely well. Clayton referees; Patrick, who had an Olympic trial for diving, has to swim twice. Despite this his team just loses, to shrieks of excitement all around. The Americans sunbathing round the pool look on in amazement. 'I never knew the British could be so overly extrovert,' says a fat Texan lady.

Sunday 23 June

Nightfall. After a pulverizing afternoon's shooting, thunder and lightning are rolling round the valley. In our rooms we get shocks from everything, taps, plugs, light switches, even the fridge. We hardly have time to change before rushing out to a barbecue.

The setting is perfect, huge stars peer through the palm trees, but the weather seems to have affected all of us. Everyone is snappy, and during the evening Patrick is so rude to the Ranger, an ageing Medallion Man called Caesar who is not entirely sober, that Caesar refuses to relinquish the $2,000 deposit given him by Sebastian to allow us to shoot in Death Valley. 'You can come back any time,' Caesar tells Sebastian, 'but don't bring that basstard, Lichfield.'

Tempers are slightly doused by a riotous drive home in a buggy which goes through several sprinklers. Anguished cries of 'My hair, my hair,' echo through the sooty black night.

Collapse into bed long after midnight. It seems only seconds later I am woken by a nauseatingly cheerful voice saying: 'Good morning, this is 3.15 a.m. and your wake-up call.' Like a zombie I stagger out of bed, pull on my clothes, and hump my suitcase out to the Winnebago. In the moonlight, the fringed tassels of the tamarisk trees sway milkily in the warm breeze. Summer lightning crackles round the mountains.

'This is effing crazy,' moans Noel, going by holding his head with one hand.

Pedro, the rock on which we build our shoot, who is quietly loading the Winnebago, helps me with my suitcase.

'Will you marry me when I grow up?' I ask.

'I'm afraid there's rather a long queue, dear,' says Clayton, who can be seen combing his eyebrows through an open bedroom door.

Aysha appears in her doorway. 'Will someone give me a hand?' she says querulously. Paula leaps forward and carries her cases.

Jackie does a spot check under everyone's beds to see if we have left anyone behind.

'Where's Patrick?' asks someone as we set off in the Winnebago.

'I should think he's rather poorly,' says Jackie.

'Good-bye Feeling-Like-Death Valley,' I mutter.

Next moment a mobile wardrobe has crashed to the ground. 'Someone's dropped an earring,' says Clayton. We all giggle and feel better.

Summer lightning is snaking along the hills after us, highlighting now a pink peak, now a green, now a gold. We are on our way to Utah, via Las Vegas, and going to shoot in some sand dunes on the way. After twenty-five miles we pass the film crew looking disconsolate. A suitcase has fallen off the top of their car on the way from Death Valley. They have to go back and look for it, and consequently miss the best row of the week.

Like *Pilgrim's Progress*, we have left Death Valley only to enter the Plain of Disenchantment. The Country Squire turns purposefully off the road, and sets off over rolling dunes. The Winnebago follows gallantly, but sinks deeper and deeper into the sand. As it lurches more and more drunkenly, I feel steadily sicker. Repeated urgent messages are sent to the Country Squire on our walkie-talkie, begging it to stop. Terse messages come back for us to soldier on. 'Mind the merchandise,' yells Chalky as a sleeping Gloria falls off her chair. Fridge and mobile wardrobe are only saved from following her just in time. We are well into the desert now, with

Cabals form in rooms.

sand dunes rising on all sides. In the distance a pink mountain is lit on one side by lightning and the other by the rising sun; the clouds are deep indigo trimmed with gold.

In no mood for aesthetic appreciation, as the Winnebago grinds to a halt I leap out and am very sick behind some tumbleweed. 'Quick, photograph her, Chalks,' yells Noel. I return to find that Pedro, the angelic, the equable, has finally flipped his lid and is screaming at Patrick, Noel and Sebastian. We all then set to, to push the Winnebago.

'This is the way we took to Tobruk,' says Noel, trying to see the bright side as the sand swirls and the wheels whirr impotently.

'We lost Tobruk, you berk,' snaps Sebastian.

'But we re-took it later,' says Noel triumphantly.

'Push,' orders Patrick in his Monty voice.

We push, and push, and push. Suddenly the Winnebago lurches forward, and we all fall flat on our faces. Bad will is absolutely rampant. I stump off to interview some desert rats, which, according to the guidebook, are common in the area. I wonder if they'll wear long shorts, like those German sightseers. Only Clayton is happy, and transfixed by the scenery: 'It's *Florence of Arabia* all over again,' he sighs.

The Modules, as Noel calls them, are now sitting in a sulky circle, saying they are fed up, as clouds gather menacingly on the horizon. Even darling sunny Paula for once has lost her high spirits. 'Hope it rains,' she mutters, 'and holds up his rotten pictures.'

'Patrick doesn't like me,' says Aysha.

'It's their attitude,' says Gloria crossly. 'Models may have been thick in the old days, but we're fed up with being treated as though we haven't any brains. Telling us not to sunbathe, as if we would in this heat.'

'This is the worst trip I've ever been on,' says Paula.

Aysha stuns us by saying that as well as her headache, her tummy-ache and her cystitis, she's been bleeding for two weeks.

Then suddenly — never more like the quality of mercy — it starts to rain. Blissfully we stretch out on the sand. The dunes too are beautiful. Rippling like ivory silk against the grooved dark blue mountains behind, they look as youthful as a baby held up against the wrinkled cheeks of its grandmother.

'You've farted, Noel.' Patrick's voice rings out over the sand.

'I bleeding 'aven't. If I fart, I go away to fart,' grumbles Noel.

Finally the rain stops, the clouds roll back, and a rainbow soars out of the purple mountains.

Paula starts to clap. 'What an excellent, excellent rainbow.'

'Awesome to the max,' says Sebastian.

Half an hour later, the sun is caressing the dunes and a slight breeze endlessly shifting them. Gloria is being photographed dancing down a ridge; she looks like a sand sprite. 'Don't fall,' bellows Patrick for the umpteenth time.

'I said I'm not going to fall, and that's that,' Gloria screams back at him.

'This is the worst trip I've ever been on,' she says as she stalks back to the Winnebago.

We breakfast at the next-door town.

Patrick and Noel aren't speaking either.

'Violence is not the answer,' mutters Noel, shaking his head, 'but it's a very good start.' He has fastened the handle of his spectacles back on again with black gaffer tape.

Pedro orders, 'Bacon and eggs and English muffins.'

'I'd have thought you'd had enough crumpet already,' says Chalky.

Patrick is beadily watching Noel trying to eat scrambled eggs. 'Why's your hand shaking so much?' he demands. 'My hands don't shake.'

'That's because *you* don't have to work with people like you,' says Noel.

Patrick howls with laughter, and the row is at an end. Over and over again, Patrick reminds me of Goldsmith's description of Garrick:

He cast off his friends like a huntsman his pack
For he knew when he pleased he could whistle
    them back.

Aware of having taken a great shot in the dunes, he is absolutely sweet for the rest of the day, sorry that I've been sick, and insisting that I travel in the Country Squire with him and Sebastian. As we proceed towards Vegas, at a funereal pace of 55 m.p.h. so as not to exceed the speed limit, the scrubby countryside looks as though it hasn't shaved for a week, and Joshua

Patrick about to be in hot water again.

trees raise two fingers to a leaden sky.

If the dunes were Disenchantment Plain, Vegas is Prodigal City. After the stark intransigence of Death Valley, its vulgarity is appalling and intrusive. 'Million dollar craps tournament. Nevada's loosest slots. See the Grand Canyon 50% discount. Honeymoon Motel, bring your dog, colour t.v. in every room,' scream the billboards. Johnny Mathis is singing at Caesar's Palace. Hector Macho CoMacho is boxing. In the gift shops you can buy towels saying: 'Ashes to Ashes, Dust to Dust, if it wasn't for women your ding dong would rust.'

We have a jolly lunch at the MGM Gambling Hall, and watch balding crones with spiky hair carrying their money in ice-cream tubs and clawing at the one-armed bandits like sleepwalkers.

Leaving Nevada, we drive on to Utah, land of industry and temperance. The landscape deepens to burgundy. As we cross the Virgin River into Indian territory, vast brooding temples of crimson rock look down as disapprovingly as dowagers. Ever changing as the light alters, they seem to have a life of their own. One can understand exactly why the Indians were animists, who believed all matter, including rock formations, had souls and could move of their own will. Whichever way you look, rock faces seem to be watching you.

We stop for the night at St George, a Mormon town with an air of prosperity and a Persil-white temple stabbing the sky, where we find the film crew waiting, despondent at the loss of both a suitcase and a day's shooting.

Soon the Winnebago party arrives in raging spirits. They have had a marvellous day in Vegas, but made a predictably British fuss at a place called Circus Circus where they found a kangaroo in weight-lifter's clothes being forced to box with a dwarf. Turning on the manager, they complained bitterly at how sick it was, whereupon, thus encouraged, the kangaroo proceeded to lay out the dwarf and then the referee. 'This is simply the best trip we've ever been on,' chorus the models ecstatically. 'Isn't Patrick *absolutely* wonderful!'

Ricocheting from euphoria when he's done a good shot to despair that he hasn't got enough in the can, every evening Patrick sticks the latest Polaroids into a scrap-book, and pores over them endlessly. He already has about eleven good pictures for the Calendar, he says. Not until he has sixteen will he relax. Under today's Polaroid of Gloria dancing down the sand dune he has written *Gloria in Excelsis*. He says she moves better than any model he's ever photographed.

Utah is dry, but Sebastian, who could get blue blood out of a stone, finds us some decent wine and we dine in a Mexican restaurant. The Mormons may not smoke, or drink tea, coffee or alcohol, but they're sure into sex. At the next table a disgustingly ugly, fresh-faced couple, both seriously overweight, devour strawberry ice-cream and each other throughout dinner.

In the lobby of the hotel is a leaflet telling you what videos can be hired. One of them is *Greystoke*, showing a picture of a vast grey castle. 'That's my brother-in-law's house,' says Patrick.

Tuesday morning 25 June

We all shiver in temperatures of 100 degrees. But blissfully, I have ankles back again. Just as we are leaving, Jackie slams the tailgate of the Country Squire not realizing that a suitcase is sticking out. The next moment, the hotel car-park is covered with green glass as the back window shatters.

With a black plastic bag instead of a back window, Sebastian, Patrick and I drive through Zion National Park. *You are entering 160 million years of natural history*, says a large sign. Certainly this is the most staggering place I have ever seen. You feel like an ant at the foot of Guildford Cathedral as massive heroic cliffs, the colour of dried blood, soar up and up and up, with a black fringing of volcanic lava and a crew-cut of pines on the top.

As the red road winds in and out of rose-red caverns measureless to man, Sebastian and I go into an orgy of 'awesomes'. Patrick, however, looks out of the window without enthusiasm. 'Not very good tank country,' he says. 'Did you know that exactly 109 years ago today, Custer had his last stand at the Little Big Horn?'

'Sounds like a piece in *Penthouse*,' says Sebastian.

Patrick then proceeds to tell us how his great-grandmother dropped a baby in the drawing-room and rang for a maid to pick it up.

Paula takes a swig.

As we come out of Zion, the rock changes yet again. Layer upon layer of sandstone, like the crêpe-ing on old ladies' thighs, rises sheer to form the canyon walls. Now we are driving through a fertile plain with sand the colour of lobster bisque and eau-de-Nil scrub. Every car we overtake is going at a decorous 55 miles an hour and has '*I love the Bible*' stickers on the back window.

Suddenly the daunting magnitude of Zion Park and the respectability of being in a dry state get to us, and we pour ourselves vast vodkas and tonics and knock them back, Sebastian negotiating hairpin bends with one hand as we drive along, not wearing seat belts and wildly exceeding the speed limit. Utah affects one like that.

'Is the mushroom soup home-made?' asks Jackie at lunch.

'Half and half,' replies the waitress.

In the afternoon we drive on to Lake Powell, Arizona, a vast man-made lake surrounded by extraordinary gold and terracotta rocks, and go slap into another row. We are to spend the next five days here, and Patrick takes one look at the Marina Motel into which we are booked, which is swarming with tourists and sailing types, and says he wants to stay at the much quieter Four Seasons Hotel up the road.

The film crew, headed by Clive, declare UDI and decide to stay at the Marina, saying they don't mind the tourists and they want to film 'in a bay-type situation'.

'Reminds him of Leigh-on-Sea,' mutters Patrick. 'I'll let his tyres down again if he's not careful.'

It is only when the rest of us are safely checked into the Four Seasons that we discover there is no bar and the bomb-site on the right of the building is the dining-room in the making. Sebastian goes wearily off in search of booze.

Matters are not improved by the fact that Lake Powell in the middle of the afternoon looks perfectly frightful – particularly after the heroic splendour of Zion. The terracotta rock and royal-blue water seem unutterably commonplace by comparison. Poor Noel, who came here on a recce a month ago and recommended the place, is seriously worried, particularly as Jackie and the models have been winding him up in the Winnebago.

'Lovely modern town, Noel,' says Jackie.

'Lovely pylons,' says Gloria.

'Like the power station,' says Paula.

'Lovely Macdonalds,' says Aysha.

Poor Noel, who has put gaffer tape on the other side of his spectacles to even them up, is massaging his face. 'Perhaps I was seriously drunk when I came here,' he says in a worried voice. 'It seemed wonderful at the time, but I could have been wrong. I'm sure there are places without pylons round here. We can always get an effing boat, and go out, and fink, and wait for inspiration to come.'

Patrick, who is a very kind man when it matters, tries to take Noel's mind off the problem by insisting he watch Wimbledon. McEnroe is playing McNamara. Noel, settling into a chair, says he used to play ping-pong with Ann Haydon Jones.

Clive, understandably frantic at having missed nearly two days' shooting in transit, wants more material for *The Big Heat* and persuades them to go out on a recce. I wander off to gossip to Jackie and then have a sleep, when Clive rings up and orders me to come along on the recce too. Feel very, very sulky.

At sunset Noel is totally vindicated – the rocks softened to rose-red, the lake to an Arctic kingfisher-blue, are unbelievably beautiful. Patrick, however, who wants all the Calendar pictures to look parched, harsh, and thirsty, wants to avoid filming water at all costs. He and Noel argue.

Clive bangs on the window. 'While you are discussing the merits of what you're going to do, can you all get out of the car, so we can shoot you?' he says pointedly.

The row continues out of the car, and increases in ferocity. Noel leads us off to another part of the lake which he has recce'd and which he thinks would be good for a shot. As we crash down a rocky track, the Country Squire loses its exhaust and sustains several huge dents in the side. With the back window gone and a disgusting mess of egg-white all over the bonnet, it is looking distinctly the worse for wear.

As we get out to assess the merits of the place Noel has recommended, Patrick promptly trips over an empty bottle of some American liqueur called Thunderbird lying in the sand.

'You can tell Noel's been here once,' he says.

Noel lends two hands.

'You can tell Noel's been here twice,' I say as I trip over another bottle.

'You can tell he's been here *three times*,' says Sebastian, as he finds a third in a tamarisk bush.

The three of us collapse in childish giggles. None of this, of course, can the film crew shoot. Quite understandably, Clive looks very boot-faced.

On the way home, Clive says he hopes he will be able to have a lot of my time tomorrow, as the film crew only have two days left before they go back to England.

At drinks in Patrick's room after dinner, I very injudiciously say that I'm fed up with being pursued by the film crew, that I have nothing intelligent to say to them, that I want to be left alone to write my book, and that absolutely no fee has been negotiated for making the video. Everyone joins in and has a good bitch about the film crew, particularly about Clive. Except Noel, who sticks up for them and walks out.

Wednesday 26 June

Restaurant-less at the Four Seasons, we breakfast at the Marina. Patrick looks sourly at seriously overweight and yelling Americans going by in shorts, and says Jocelyn Stevens once sent him to Miami to photograph the 'real people'. After two days he sent Jocelyn a telegram saying, 'There aren't any.'

Sebastian has been watching bowling on television and heard a commentator saying of one of the bowlers: 'I think he's about to be awfully awesome.'

Everyone argues noisily about where we are going to shoot next. A boat trip to some distant rocks is suggested. 'I'm not coming,' says Jackie flatly, 'I get sea-sick on the Serpentine.'

Aysha, as well as bleeding, cystitis, headache and tummy-ache, now has a paralysed arm and diarrhoea. Jackie insists on taking her to the doctor.

'I hope it won't cost too much,' says Aysha in alarm.

'Not unless you have major heart surgery,' says Sebastian gravely.

Aysha turns green.

Darling Clayton buys me a black T-shirt from the hotel shop with *Awesome* written in shock-ing-pink across the bosom.

Hideously embarrassing situation after breakfast. Clive asks me if he can have a word, and bears me off to his room, which is as neat as his figure. He then tells me that Noel rang him at 12.30 when he was fast asleep, and told him we were all saying frightful things about him, particularly me. 'Jilly's so fed up,' Noel evidently said, 'she's threatening to go home.'

Noel had then proceeded to ring up Unipart, who presumably had only just got into their offices in England, and told them everything was disintegrating and the whole shoot falling apart. As a result, Clive was then woken at four o'clock in the morning by the client asking what the hell was going on?

Blushing like a discomfited beetroot, I stammer that no one was really being beastly about Clive, but, with a pack like we are, we obviously have a rotation of scapegoats, and last night it was his turn to be the fall guy. It was all my fault, I confess, because I happened to be feeling fed up about not having time to concentrate on my book, and *of course* we all adore him.

Clive then says he's tried to be pleasant over the years, but that I have been seduced like everyone else by Lichfield's damn charm, and we all hang on to his every word like lackeys.

Say meekly that I will spent the rest of the day interviewing Clayton, the models, and probably Patrick, for the video, and endeavouring to scintillate. Desperate to change the subject, I ask Clive if he's swum in the lake.

He laughs, and says: 'No, but I felt like jumping in it at four o'clock this morning.'

Aysha has been to the doctor who has given her some all-purpose cream, and she has perked up considerably. She perks up even more when she hears Patrick is going to photograph her this afternoon.

Interview her, Paula and Gloria round the pool. They are incredibly articulate, particularly Gloria. They say their parents – after initial embarrassment at seeing their offspring without clothes in various magazines and catalogues – are very proud, and support them all the way. They also say their boyfriends are very proud of them and never jealous. Remembering Brett le Stafford's nine telephone calls a day to Aysha, I think this may be whistling in the dark.

Meanwhile the rest of the crew are transfixed by a fifteen-year-old girl lying by the pool in a

I show off my awesome T-shirt to Clayton, Jackie and Noel.

Sulks in the sands: me
and Aysha

bikini, with multi-braces on her teeth and four perfect finger-mark bruises on the outside of either thigh. As her fat father approaches, she hastily covers up the bruises with a towel.

'When I was fourteen,' confides Aysha, 'I once had love bites all over my neck, and couldn't sit down for a week.'

We look at her perplexed.

'Because my Mum gave me such a hiding,' she says.

Noel, who is not popular for ringing up Unipart, is frozen out by Patrick at lunch. As he desperately tries to wheedle himself back into Patrick's good books, I am reminded once again of Falstaff, pleading with Hal that if he banishes 'plump Jack' he will 'banish all the world'. Patrick, however, refuses to be mollified.

Thursday 27 June

Blissful morning off. Patrick has agreed to take portraits of everyone. As a Lichfield portrait normally costs £1,000 a throw, the models are in a high state of excitement. 'Shall I wear my diamanté necklace?' asks Aysha.

Patrick creates the perfect studio by using one of Noel's sheets thrown over the Winnebago as a back-drop. Chalky and Pedro hold up reflectors like great white hoops, Sebastian lounges on top of the Winnebago holding a large umbrella. 'The light is so good,' explains Chalky, 'that British crews often fly out here to do entire catalogues, so they don't have to waste hours fiddling about with lighting or spend fortunes on model fees as they wait for the sun to come out.'

A television crew from Utah have just arrived at the hotel. They simply cannot figure why these mad Englishmen should turn their backs on a staggering view of miles of red rock gashed with ice-blue water, and photograph against the Winnebago. Their leader, a six-foot-four blond with massive thighs, called John, says he comes from Salt Lake City. Clayton, who is deciding whether to wear kingfisher-blue or white in the photograph, eyes him speculatively.

Having averaged about two hours sleep a night and a third of a bottle of vodka a day on this trip, I look simply frightful, with little white-rat red eyes. You could also drive to Salt Lake City on my red veins. But Clayton gets to work with his paintbrushes and pencils, smudging, moulding, embellishing, and manages to make a silk purse out of a very ancient sow's ear, and lop at least twenty-five years off my age.

Such is Patrick's genius that we all emerge in the Polaroids far more beautiful than we've ever done before – except Noel, who has not yet been forgiven for sneaking by Patrick, and who looks rather like an Idaho potato that's been attacked by a Colorado beetle.

Unable to find the girls or Noel, we go to lunch. Angry at such insubordination, Patrick is even further irritated to discover that Noel has borne the girls off for a drink with the film crew at the Marina.

Patrick may be the shepherd whistling the orders, but Sebastian is the sheepdog rounding us up, getting us into hotels and out of trouble. He has a wonderful calm and kindness that has all the girls, including me, half in love with him. As blond and equable as Jackie is dark and volatile, they make the ideal couple.

This afternoon he has hired a huge two-storey motorboat called *Ethel* for the afternoon, so Patrick can shoot the models on the far side of the lake. Big John from Salt Lake City has, to Clayton's delight, asked if he can come along too, with his camera. Clive's film crew are off home in the morning, so they are desperately anxious for a good afternoon's work as well.

Patrick is miked up, so am I, but over the waistband of my skirt so that I don't get prickly heat. Patrick wants to gossip, so he promptly unplugs us both. Two seconds later, Clive whisks down the boat and re-plugs me. 'We'd like you to remain plugged in,' he says reprovingly.

So on the blink, I am terrified I will say something indiscreet. Patrick is still ignoring Noel, who gets more and more extravagant in his clowning as *Ethel* sets sail across the Prussian-blue water. Soon huge gold temples, pink arches, igloos, and caves are rearing up to left and right. Jackie, who has forgotten her seasickness, and I sunbathe topless, with Sebastian standing between us and the film crew. Everyone is happy, particularly when we reach a plateau of rock layered brown and singed like a Pavlova cake left overnight in the Aga, which is perfect for shooting. *Ethel*'s anchor is dropped.

Patrick has even forgiven Noel.

'It's good to see you smile again, Guv'nor,' says Noel.

We are just wading ashore, when suddenly

The camera crew return to *Ethel*.

Jackie and Sebastian

Patrick catches sight of the film crew's clipboard. They have changed the name of their film from *The Big Heat* to *The Big Heap*, to show what they think of us. Like a maddened bull, Patrick goes berserk, ripping out his and my microphones and ordering Clive and his team off the shoot. The whole boat is in an uproar; any second I expect to hear the hissing of cutlasses. The language is so blue, poor *Ethel* is putting her rudder over her portholes. Big John from Salt Lake City looks on in amazement. The half-moon, showing one smudgy eye, peers cautiously round a curtain of blue sky.

As the camera crew drag their bags over the rocks and set up the shot to photograph Paula, Clive considers the possibility of making one of his crew swim the ten miles back to the Marina to charter a rescue-boat. Then, having already lost a suitcase earlier in the week, decides he can't afford to lose an employee as well.

'What the hell did you have to *do* that for?' I scream at him. 'We were all so happy.'

Clive's eternal smile has for once slipped like a stage moustache. For five years, he says wearily, he has put up with Patrick's arrogance. Calling the film *The Big Heap* was a small symbol of rebellion.

'But a bloody silly one, if he won't let you film any more.'

'Patrick actually called Paul, my sound man, "Cloth Ears" the other day.'

'He didn't,' I say, wearily.

'All the models are fed up with Patrick,' says Clive, getting out the wooden spoon.

'Rubbish,' I say, 'they adore him.'

Bleached tumbleweed floats across the lake like a succession of Arthur Scargill wigs, as I join the camera crew. As Paula takes up her position, no one is entirely concentrating. One by one they sidle up to me, and ask what did Clive say? 'He didn't.' 'I didn't.' 'I really *really* didn't.' 'The bastard.' 'It's *simply* not true!'

A massively fat Mormon in a red rubber waistcoat wades over, and Paula has to put on her clothes and pretend once more to be studying rock formations. The fat Mormon tells us *Better Homes and Gardens* are doing a spread on his family reunion. Forty-five grown-ups and children are staying on a houseboat across the creek. His parents had nine children, and they had thirty children between them.

'Must be hell at Christmas,' I say.

Time is running short, so Jackie asks him if he or his family will mind Paula posing nude? Sweating with excitement, he says no one will mind, least of all him.

A paddle-steamer comes by, coloured flags flying, a huge scarlet wheel churning up the water. Dispiritedly, for want of anything better to do, the film crew film it.

Patrick has finished photographing Paula. He is so delighted with the shot that, with one of his staggering *volte-faces*, he relents and says Clive can film the last shot of the day.

We then move on to another plateau – and you have the ridiculous situation of two crows sitting on a blonde peak, watching the film crew filming Big John from Salt Lake City, who is filming Chalky, who is taking a black and white photograph of Patrick, aided by Pedro, photographing Gloria, who is posing in the costume that Jackie built.

Sebastian, a fellow Pisces and hating rows as much as I do, has a wonderful ability to make things seem normal. Sidling up, he says he thinks Clayton has a serious crush on Thunderthighs from Salt Lake City. 'Like Oliver Twist asking for Mormon,' I say.

Gloria sits on the rocks in the lotus position, a waterfall of grey tassels plunging between her legs, gazing haughtily out of a sea-green head-dress that would make anyone else look silly. Paula, as joyous as a water baby, swims naked in the lake. Aysha sunbathes on the deck. Clayton is gazing at Thunderthighs in such wonder that Sebastian throws a prickly pear at him.

The sun is sinking, putting an ice-blue rinse on the lake. I have run out of superlatives. How can I possibly describe such ravishing rocks? I ask in despair. Paul, Clive's sound man, who is hovering, ponders for a second. 'It's like Valhalla built for the Gods by the giants Fasolt and Fafner,' he says, getting it in one. 'That wonderful moment at the end of *Rheingold*, when the Gods pass over the rainbow bridge and enter into the castle at sunset.'

We all gaze at him in awe – definitely not Cloth Ears. And I suddenly realize all the rocks we have seen have been just like a succession of massive opera sets.

The lights begin to twinkle from the rocks, the long day wanes, the slow moon climbs. By some

The film crew.

miracle *Ethel* gets us back to the Marina without further explosions. As it is late, we eat Macdonald hamburgers round the hotel swimming-pool. The setting is perfect, with huge stars reflected dimly in the silken green water and everyone looking bronzed and handsome after a day in the sun. We are all on our best behaviour, determined not to rock the boat on the film crew's last night.

Then we all troop into the television room, and watch the video of Clive's film of last year's Calendar shoot in Bali on a big screen. Entitled *The Making of a Model*, it is to be networked in July.

The film I suppose is well made, but I absolutely detest it. Clive has entirely angled it from the viewpoint of a wingeing model who was picked to go on the shoot as a total amateur and loathed every minute of it. She appears to have hated everyone and never stopped grumbling from the moment she left England. She is even filmed throwing up in a stream.

'The reason we didn't use her at the beginning of the shoot,' whispers Patrick, 'is because she was an amateur, and at that stage you always use the professionals because you want to get something in the can.'

The commentary by Michael Parkinson is curiously lifeless and flat. All the models come across as bellyaching little nitwits, and there is practically no praise for the fantastic hard work, the dedication, and the loving attention to detail of Patrick, Noel, Clayton, Sebastian, Jackie, Pedro and Chalky. If *The Big Heap* this afternoon was Clive's little rebellion, this is a hatchet-job on a group of people I've really grown to adore. I walk out of the room, go to bed, and cry my eyes out.

Within two minutes there is a thundering on the door. It is the three models. They come and mop me up, and sit on my bed and say the film was *ghastly*, and it made the models out to be absolute twits, and they've just given Clive an earful.

Two minutes later they are joined by Sebastian and Jackie, who also mop me up and say the film was awful, tasteless and boring, and they've given Clive an earful too.

Two minutes later, Patrick rolls up and says: 'You are an old ham, Cooper,' and do we know that England are 210 all out, and Australia are

134 for four?

'We've got about fourteen serious pictures in the can,' he says. 'Tomorrow we want a real cracker.'

Friday 28 June

God, I want to go home. Am suddenly desperately missing Leo and the children and the dogs and England. Turning on the television, I discover the American hostages are still trapped in Beirut. I have become so caught up in the Unipart dramas, I have forgotten the rest of the world exists.

Feeling I need to distance myself from the lot of them, and because I don't want to confront Clive and tell him how much I hate his film, I stay in my room typing all day. Only to be interrupted by the models and most of the crew banging on my door and asking if they can borrow tranquillizers. At this rate, I'll have to have another canister airlifted in by British Caledonian.

Jump out of my skin as Clive appears through the French windows of my room. He is just off to the airport. His mahogany legs in the inevitable snow-white shorts are umber after yesterday's boat trip. Instead of saying 'Anyone for tennis?' he asks what I thought of his film. Stammer that it was probably excellent technically, but very biased against Patrick's mob. Clive shrugs his shoulders and says it was made through the eyes of one particular model.

'There is no truth,' I say sadly, quoting Edith Sitwell, 'only points of view.'

Clive's voice thickens slightly as he says he hopes he's going to get a look at what I've written before it goes to the printers.

I shake my head. 'This is going to be *my* small symbol of rebellion,' I say gently.

Later in the day, trying to get some sense of perspective, I talk to Chalky, who like me has been watching and recording the whole thing. 'There haven't been any more rows this year than any other,' he says. 'You'll always get tensions with a small group of people. The film crew are really lovely guys. They were just the butt for tensions that had to come out somewhere. It's good to have someone we can unite against, and hate.'

I spend the rest of the afternoon reading Trollope. Sebastian, who has also had enough,

I interview models round the pool for the film crew.

Bat woman

borrows a copy of Jane Gardham's short stories and takes a rowing-boat out on the lake, hoping for a couple of hours' peace. Alas, he is permanently interrupted by kindly Americans stopping their boats to see if he's all right, and exhorting him to have a nice day.

The Winnebago, about the only thing on this trip not to have thrown a serious moody, gives up the ghost and is towed off to the menders.

We walk to dinner in a splendid Wild West Saloon. Beefy men in stetsons gaze at the models. I seem to have lost my appetite, and can do no justice to the four dinosaur ribs each carrying about 2lbs of red meat, and the potato field of French fries, that arrive on my plate.

Patrick, who has a strong streak of Professor Higgins in his nature and believes people should improve themselves, is encouraging Paula to have clam chowder.

'I'd throw up,' she says.

'What would happen', asks Patrick with some asperity, 'if you were having dinner with the President?'

'I'd have to sooffer,' says Paula.

Patrick tells me that on the French Calendar shoot they had a chef called Angus, known as Agnes, who cooked on roller-skates wearing pink satin trousers, and who served up both brains and calves' heads, which the models devoured with huge enjoyment without realizing what they were eating.

As we are leaving, he makes a serious attempt to bring out Aysha. 'Have you enjoyed the trip?' he asks.

'Yes, I suppose so,' she says without enthusiasm.

'You realize you're in Red Indian country. Have you had a chance to look at anything Indian?'

'No.'

'Haven't you read any of the guidebooks?'

'No, I've been reading my romantic novel, *The Purity and the Passion*.'

Patrick stalks off, shaking his head in bewilderment. 'We had a model in South Carolina who stayed in her room knitting all day,' he says.

A punishing last day's shooting is planned. We will drive to Monument Valley, where John Ford made all his movies, have lunch on the way, dinner probably on the way back, then get up at five to start the journey home.

Seven a.m., Saturday 29 June

Jackie is telephoning home, shouting particularly loudly because the call is long distance and she is talking to the South American *au pair*, who has toothache. 'No, there are no dentistas open tilla Monday,' she yells. 'You'll just hava to lumpa it.'

Patrick, who is about to be interviewed by Big John from Salt Lake City, is frantically emptying a whole bottle of blue drops into his eyes. It seems monstrously unfair that men look battered and sexy when they're tired, and women just look awful.

The Winnebago is working again – it was evidently pre-igniting in the heat and it had a flat battery. Pedro, the saintly, the even-tempered, who hasn't put a foot wrong this trip, collects it from the garage. Backing it into a virtually empty hotel car-park, he goes slap into the side of the Country Squire. Once again the tarmac is covered in green glass. Everyone screams with laughter, except Sebastian who sits with his head in his hands. 'Why don't you back it into Noel's room and finish it off altogether, Pedro?' he says.

The garage mechanics who have just mended the Winnebago shake with silent laughter at this strange English team hell-bent on playing dodg'em cars, and give us a second plastic bag to tape up the side window of the Country Squire.

As we set off to Monument Valley, I talk to Noel. 'You can't argue with Patrick,' he says, 'you have to coax him. I just walk away on a shoot, and when he looks round, I say why don't you just shoot a roll *this* way? It hasn't helped him having the film crew around. If he's miked up he starts to perform, play the general, and shout around at the company just to show he's in command. You can understand, though, why he gets uptight. At the end of the day the Calendar is Patrick's work, and he'll be judged on it.'

Up at the front of the Winnebago, the models are all asleep. Paula, with her knickers down to avoid elastic marks, shows a bum as smooth and brown as a conker. I am not envious of their beauty any more, only of their ability to sleep.

I didn't believe there could possibly be any other kind of rock, but Monument Valley is

Paula keeps out of trouble.

different again. Out of flat stretches of lettuce-green scrub rise huge browny-red masses of sandstone, like medieval fortresses glaring at one another, or like chess pieces on a vast billiard table. Some are shaped like stovepipe hats; two crouch facing each other like hares; others are like giant upside-down teeth that have been torn out by the roots.

'Makes a chap feel very inadequate,' says Chalky, photographing a succession of massive phallic symbols.

'Overly awesome – Stone-minge, in fact,' says Sebastian.

Everyone in the Winnebago is wild with excitement, except Aysha who is still sleeping peacefully.

This is Navajo territory, and we have no licence to shoot. Paula is just stripping off behind the Winnebago when an exceptionally stroppy Red Indian Ranger roars up and orders us off the property. No amount of sweet-talking can win him round. Any moment the Country Squire will be full of arrows, so we move out of the reservation, and Patrick decides to shoot on a flat red rock with the phalluses and torn-out teeth in the distance.

Paula is soon posing in an extraordinary full-length green mackintosh cape. Frantically Jackie and I plait Aysha's hair, while Clayton slaps on war-paint and kohls her eyes.

'I'm so tired, I've got diarrhoea, and I've jagged my big toenail so it's sticking into the other one, have you got a plaster, Jackie?' says Aysha.

'Aysha!' yells Noel.

'I haven't got any mascara on, and my knick-knicks are falling down,' wails Aysha as she sets out, feathers dropping from her hair, like a moulting chicken.

'Might as well put mascara on an ant, when you realize how small you're going to be in these pictures, duckie,' mutters Jackie to her departing back.

Having been towed up a rock face steeper than the Eiger by Sebastian and Noel, Aysha stands dispiritedly on the top.

'Get her clothes off,' snaps Patrick, rigid with the tension of a last shot. 'And get those feathers off too, they look like long armpit hair.'

'Esher,' calls Noel, the eternal Mrs Malaprop, 'can you take off those feathers?'

We have reached the silly stage, and everyone falls about. 'Why not call her Staines, Egham or Purley, you old goat,' says Patrick.

Finally there is a last roll and a Polaroid.

'Shall we say it now?' says Noel.

'Yes,' says Patrick.

'It's all over, *it's a wrap*,' they chorus.

'Oh, I wanted to say it,' says Clayton, his eyes filling with tears.

Everyone else whoops and cheers, Paula swoops around in her mackintosh cape like Batman. Jackie, Gloria, Clayton and I do a war-dance. Then we all pose on the red rocks for a last group photograph. Back go the feathers, the beads, and the tomahawks into the dressing-up box.

On the way back to the hotel we play 'I am a Famous Person' but we are so tired we keep forgetting whom we are impersonating in the middle of a round.

'Look at that awesome sunset,' I say to Sebastian.

'I don't want to, I'm fed up to the back teeth with scenery,' he says.

Noel is behind, driving Paula and Aysha in the battered Country Squire. Seeing us all getting stuck into the vodka, he puts his foot on the accelerator.

'Please don't go so fast, Noel, my ears are popping,' pleads Aysha.

Back at the Four Seasons, we all troop off to change for dinner. Only Pedro stays behind, unloading the camera bags into his room. Orange sand is shaken out of every bit of equipment, lenses and magazines are lovingly dusted and polished with the precision of a watchmaker. Tonight, he says, he's going to take the tripod into the shower with him.

The last roll of film is also carefully wrapped in polythene and joins the other 160 precious rolls and the 133 Polaroids that have been used, in a black camera bag. This bag will not leave Pedro's side ('I even take it to the john with me on the flight') until he delivers it safely back to Lichfield Studios.

Pedro has worked for Patrick for fourteen years. 'I went for an interview, we talked for forty-five minutes and he said: Come for a month's trial. After a year I said: Have I got the job? That was fourteen years ago, it seems like fourteen months. He's got such a wonderful

Aysha moulting in Monument Valley.

personality. There are a lot of good photographers around, but none of them has Patrick's authority.'

No one has much appetite for dinner. Patrick makes a tactful speech, thanking everyone for being wonderful and being themselves. In three hours we will set out for home.

Sunday 30 June

We drive to Vegas, where we shall take a flight to Houston and then to Gatwick. Patrick sits in the back of the Country Squire and, unknown to Noel, is using the top of Noel's head as an ashtray.

At Vegas, dizzy with tiredness, we bid a fond farewell to what is left of the Country Squire. It is as hot here as it was in Death Valley. The hostages still haven't been released, so security is appallingly tight. Even worse, there is a bomb scare on our flight to Houston and fire engines are pouring on to the tarmac. Patrick, who looks much better than J.R. in a stetson, is stalking about trying to find out what is going on. Perhaps I should write a book on the difference between the American and English class system called *Ewing and Non-Ewing*.

Mercifully we get a flight to LA, and from there get on to a British Caledonian flight to Gatwick. To everyone's excitement, George Segal is on our plane. He has a charming smile, and luxuriant curls the colour of Oxford marmalade. Air-hostesses and stewards flutter around him. 'His hair used to be as grey as mine,' says Patrick dismissively.

Noel is reading the English Sundays. 'Did you know Gene Autry is the richest star in Hollywood?' he yells across George Segal's bows.

Up to the teeth, like Sebastian, with scenery, I can hardly bear to look out of the window at the Grand Canyon. Noel charges across the aisle to have a gaze and is immediately socked in the crutch by George Segal's chair going back so he can get the eight hours' beauty sleep necessary to a superstar.

Patrick, having finished reading every word on Wimbledon and the Test Match, is in a mood of self-justification. When he started photographing the Calendar in 1978, he says, he had a hankering to get away from the car calendar cliché of a lady bereft of clothes in an indeterminate setting. Every year since, the background

has become more and more important, and the Calendar has moved further and further away from the lubrication bay and into the board room.

'This year we extended it by doing some landscapes into which girls fit, maybe a bit theatrically: Gloria dancing down the dunes, Paula riding across the salt flats.' He was helped, he says, by the best team in the world, and by three wonderful models.

'What about the moody you threw on the first night, over Jackie's clothes?' I ask.

'I was wrong, but I get so knotted up. I have to please a client I can't see, and an art director. I have to say, we're using your props and your make-up to Jackie and Clayton; I have to please the models. And because they're so far away, I have to shout at them over a walkie-talkie. I'm permanently miked up by the film company, so I have to watch my language and keep my tummy in. I am increasingly conscious my wife might worry about the seamy side of calendar photography.'

He is further irritated by accusations that a member of the royal family shouldn't photograph nudes.

'Name any famous painter in the eighteenth and nineteenth centuries, they did nudes as well as faces. I was tying up the Unipart Calendar in 1981 at Nelson's home in Sicily when they asked me to photograph the royal wedding.'

I am just thinking the Lord doth protest too much, when he suddenly gives one of his schoolboy grins and says: 'Did you know when Prince Charles's son was born, the bookies gave 1000–1 on him being called Denzil?'

Raging with migraine and anti-climax now, he has twelve hours to kill before being catapulted into a work-schedule that would shatter ten photographers. It is nice to see him fall into a deep sleep.

Monday 1 July

The Uniparty is over. We exchange fond farewells at Gatwick, vowing to have lunch, to have dinner, to write, to ring. The 160 rolls of film are now on their way to London, and Patrick will have to bite his nails until 31 July, when the twelve best pictures, one for each month, are shown to Unipart.

It has been such a marvellous trip, despite the

Paula enjoying the barbecue.

POOL RULES

1. ALL PERSONS USING POOL DO SO AT OWN RISK – OWNERS & MGT. NOT RESPONSIBLE FOR ACCIDENTS OR INJURIES.

2. POOL IS FOR PRIVATE USE . . . OTHERS WITH MGT. PERMISSION ONLY.

3. NO DOGS OR CATS ALLOWED.

4. NO DRINKS OR FOOD MAY BE SERVED.

5. UNNECESSARY NOISE NOT PERMITTED AT ANY TIME.

6. AFTER USING POOL, SLIPPERS & TOWELS MUST BE USED WHEN RETURNING TO BUILDING.

7. WOMENS CAPS REQUIRED FOR LONG HAIR.

8. MGT. RESERVES RIGHT TO DENY USE OF POOL TO ANYONE AT ANY TIME.

POOL HOURS
_____ TO _____

rows, and I love them all so much, that I shed a few tears in the car going home. But never has Gloucestershire looked greener or more lovely. All the roses have waited for my return. And never have I been more pleased to see Leo, and the dogs, and talk to the children on the telephone. I can feel the guy-ropes going down. Only here lies peace after uneasy truancy.

'You were quite right about the cauldron of rows, feuds and jealousies,' I mutter as I fall into bed and sleep for eighteen hours.

Wednesday 31 July London

Arrive at Lichfield Studios for the Big Day – when the calendar photographs are to be presented to Unipart. Having heard that Patrick has done his back playing cricket – with Imran Khan no less – and been in traction for two and a half weeks, I expect him to be bowed and grey with pain. Instead he looks sensational, a stone lighter, and all bags under his eyes gone after a good rest in hospital. Noel and Pedro also have Daz-white eyeballs and concave stomachs, and smugly say they too have shed a stone since they got home.

Then the men from Unipart – Keith Russell, the marketing manager, and Alan Butler – arrive, and we all troop upstairs, falling over a charming black labrador called Jo Jo on the way. I feel really nervous for Patrick as the lights are dimmed, and we sit back to look at the chosen photographs on to a large screen.

I needn't have worried. For suddenly there are Zabriskie Point and Lake Powell and Monument Valley brought miraculously – indeed awesomely – to life. There are the wonderful stinging colours, and the models like golden creatures in fable. The salt flats look so real I can feel my eyes stinging and the sweat trickling between my shoulder-blades. And I realize that the heat, the dust, the tensions, and the feuds have given birth to one of the most marvellous sets of pictures I have ever seen – proving to anyone that photography can be an art form.

Ironically, too, the worst rows seem to have generated the best pictures: Gloria skipping down the sand dunes the day Pedro lost his temper with Patrick and I was sick behind the tumbleweed; Paula climbing up the layered Lake Powell rock trailing sunlight in her wake, photographed twenty minutes after Patrick had

ordered Clive off the shoot for calling their film *The Big Heap*.

Unipart is clearly enraptured. Even Keith Russell is shaken out of his customary sangfroid. 'They're absolutely staggering. I imagined Death Valley as nothing but skulls and horns lying in the dust.'

'It was certainly horny,' says Noel, getting the conversation back to its normal level.

Agreeing that these are easily the best photographs Patrick has ever taken, we have a drink to celebrate. Patrick, followed somewhat reluctantly by Noel and Pedro, settles for bitter lemon. Accepting a massive vodka and tonic, I vow to go on a thirty-one day post-Unipart-Calendar-Trip crash diet tomorrow.

Lichfield Studios – admiring the 1986 Unipart Calendar pictures. Noel, Ashted, Patrick minus a stone, Keith Russell of Unipart, Pedro, Me, the two Alans (Bates and Butler) of Unipart.

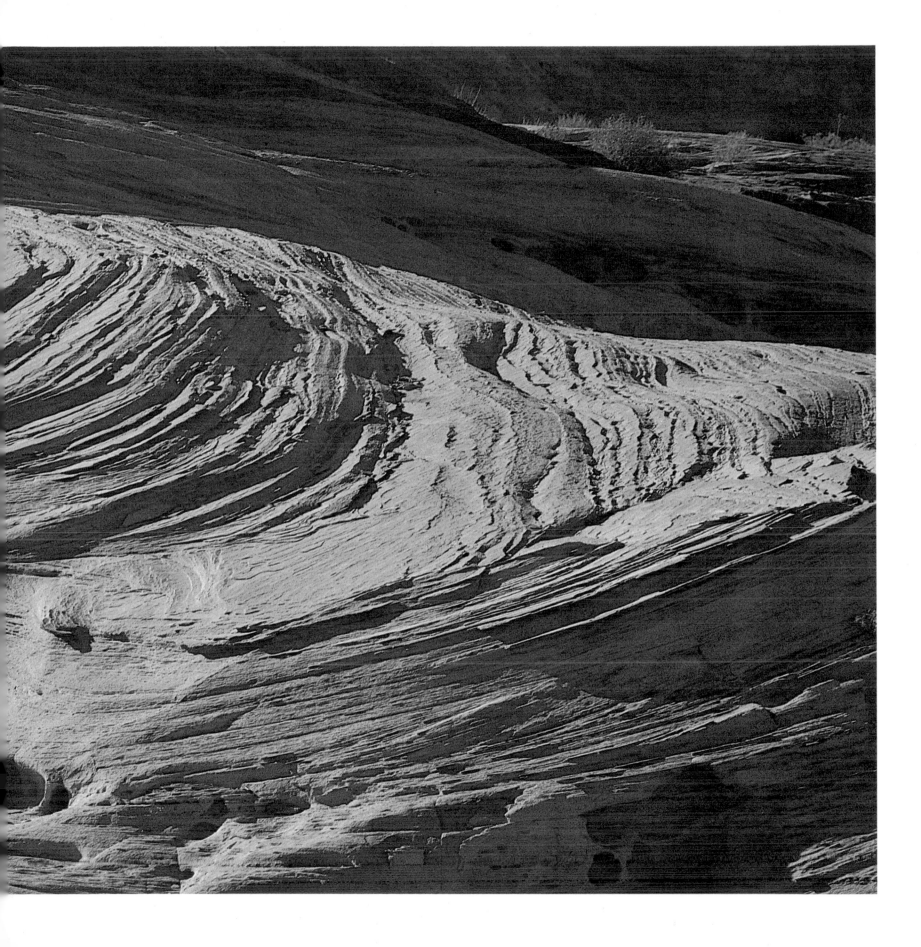

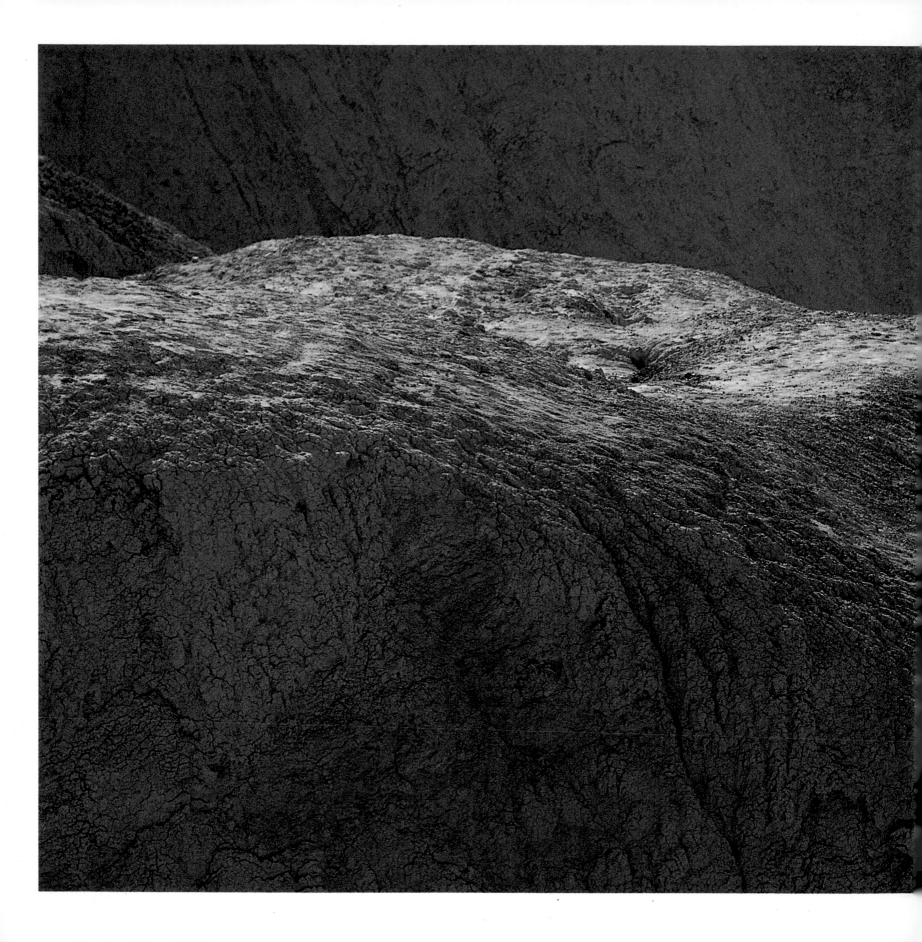

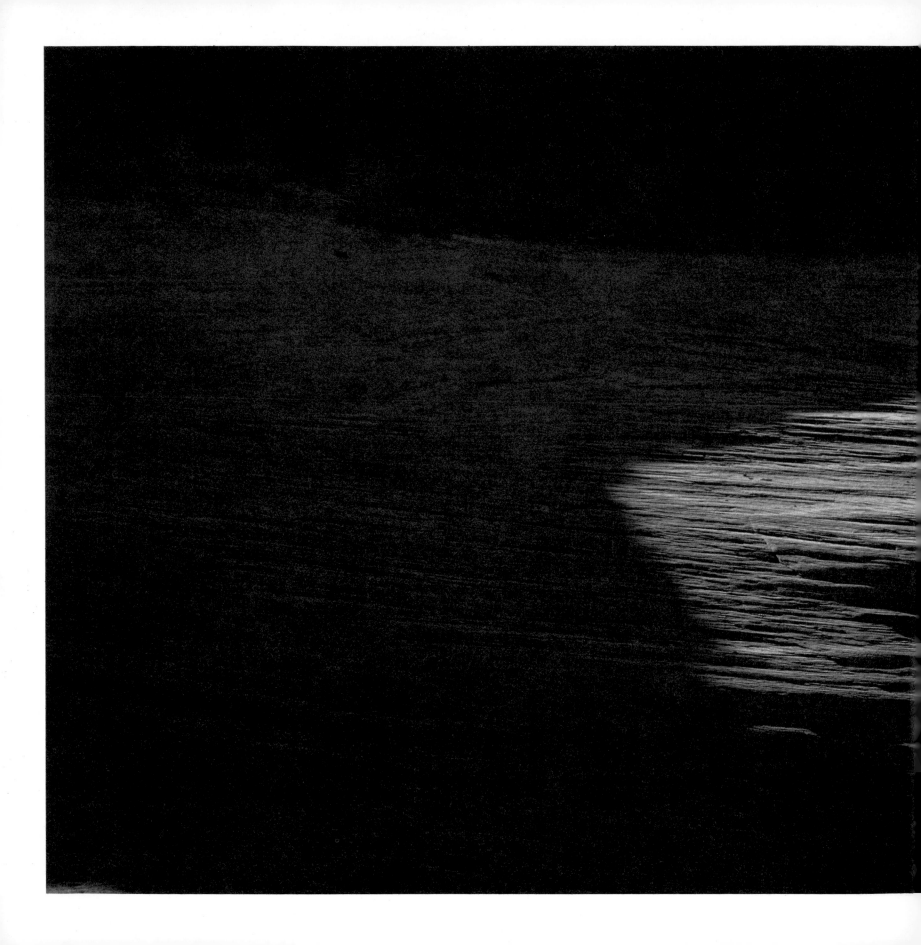